WORKING IN A LEGAL AND REGULATORY ENVIRONMENT

A HANDBOOK FOR SCHOOL LEADERS

David J. Sperry
University of Utah

EYE ON EDUCATION
6 DEPOT WAY WEST, SUITE 106
LARCHMONT, NY 10538
(914) 833–0551
(914) 833–0761 fax

Library of Congress Cataloging-in-Publication Data

Sperry, David J., 1944–
        Working in a legal and regulatory environment : a handbook
for school leaders / David J. Sperry.
        p.   cm.
        Includes bibliographical references and indexes.
        ISBN 1-883001-63-3
        1. School management and organization—Law and legisla-
tion—United States.   2. School administrators—United States— Handbooks, manuals, etc. I. Title.
KF4119.8.E3S68   1999
371.2'00973—dc21   98–41299
                                                                             CIP

10 9 8 7 6 5 4 3 2 1

Editorial and production services provided by Richard H. Adin Freelance
Editorial Services, 9 Orchard Drive, Gardiner, NY 12525 (914-883-5884)

The School Leadership Library

David A. Erlandson and Alfred P. Wilson, General Editors

The School Leadership Library, a series of 21 books, shows you what successful principals and other school leaders must know and be able to do. Grounded in best knowledge and practice, these books demonstrate best practices of effective principals. They provide recommendations which can be applied to a school leader's daily work.

Each volume includes practical materials, such as:

- checklists
- sample letters and memos
- model forms
- action plans

What should an effective principal know and be able to do? Members of the National Policy Board for Educational Administration (sponsored by NAESP, NASSP, AASA, ASCD, NCPEA, UCEA, and other professional organizations) developed a set of 21 "domains," or building blocks, that represent the essential knowledge and skills of successful principals. Each volume in this series is dedicated to explaining and applying one of these building blocks.

Contact Eye On Education for more details.

The School Leadership Library

The Functional Domains

Leadership Gary M. Crow, L. Joseph Matthews, and Lloyd E. Mccleary

Information Collection Short, Short, and Brinson, Jnr.

Problem Analysis C.M. Achilles, John Reynolds, and Susan Hoover

Judgment James Sweeney and Diana Bourisaw

Organizational Oversight Erlandson, Stark, and Ward

Implementation Anita M. Pankake

Delegation Michael Ward

The Programmatic Domains

Instruction and the Learning Environment James Keefe and John Jenkins

Staff Development Sally Zepeda

Student Guidance and Development Ward and Worsham

Measurement and Evaluation James F. Mcnamara and David A. Erlandson

Resource Allocation M. Scott Norton and Larry Kelly

The Interpersonal Domains

Motivating Others David P. Thompson

Interpersonal Sensitivity John R. Hoyle and Harrison M. Crenshaw

Oral and Nonverbal Expression Ivan Muse

Written Expression India J. Podsen, Charles Allen, Glenn Pethel, and John Waide

The Contextual Domains

Working in a Legal and Regulatory Environment: A Handbook for School Leaders David Sperry

* Other titles to follow

ACKNOWLEDGMENTS

The author would like to acknowledge and express appreciation to these individuals: Al Wilson and David Erlandson, series editors, whose patience, long suffering, and amiable spirit provided help and encouragement; Marilynn Howard for the many hours spent in typing the manuscript and developing several of the illustrations; Dale Baker, Joseph Matthews, and Danny Talbot for reading the initial manuscript and providing insightful and useful recommendations; France Rimli-Shortridge for technical assistance; Rebecca Raybould, Ph.D. candidate in Educational Leadership at the University of Utah, for assisting with various library and computer research activities; outside blind reviewers of the near-finished manuscript for their careful reading and excellent suggestions; colleagues in the Department of Educational Leadership and Policy at the University of Utah, especially Gary Crow, for encouragement and support. And, finally, the author wishes to express sincere love and appreciation to his wife, Phyllis, for her sacrifice of time and editorial assistance.

FOREWORD

The School Leadership Library was designed to show practicing and aspiring principals what they should know and be able to do to be effective leaders of their schools. The books in this series were written to answer the question, "How can we improve our schools by improving the effectiveness of our principals?"

Success in the principalship, like in other professions, requires mastery of a knowledge and skills base. One of the goals of the National Policy Board for Educational Administration (sponsored by NAESP, NASSP, AASA, ASCD, NCPEA, UCEA, and other professional organizations) was to define and organize that knowledge and skill base. The result of our efforts was the development of a set of 21 "domains," building blocks representing the core understanding and capabilities required of successful principals.

The 21 domains of knowledge and skills are organized under four broad areas: Functional, Programmatic, Interpersonal, and Contextual. They are as follows:

FUNCTIONAL DOMAINS

Leadership
Information Collection
Problem Analysis
Judgment
Organizational Oversight
Implementation
Delegation

PROGRAMMATIC DOMAINS

Instruction and the Learning
  Environment
Curriculum Design
Student Guidance and
  Development
Staff Development
Measurement and Evaluation
Resource Allocation

INTERPERSONAL DOMAINS

Motivating Others
Interpersonal Sensitivity
Oral and Nonverbal Expression
Written Expression

CONTEXTUAL DOMAINS

Philosophical and Cultural
  Values
Legal and Regulatory
  Applications
Policy and Political Influences
Public Relations

These domains are not discrete, separate entities. Rather, they evolved only for the purpose of providing manageable descriptions of essential content and practice so as to better understand the entire complex role of the principalship. Because human behavior comes in "bunches" rather than neat packages, they are also overlapping pieces of a complex puzzle. Consider the domains as converging streams of behavior that spill over one another's banks but that all contribute to the total reservoir of knowledge and skills required of today's principals.

The School Leadership Library was established by General Editors David Erlandson and Al Wilson to provide a broad examination of the content and skills in all of the domains. The authors of each volume in this series offer concrete and realistic illustrations and examples, along with reflective exercises. You will find their work to be of exceptional merit, illustrating with insight the depth and interconnectedness of the domains. This series provides the fullest, most contemporary, and most useful information available for the preparation and professional development of principals.

Scott Thomson
Executive Secretary
National Policy Board for
Educational Administration

PREFACE

A new principal has many concerns related to the implementation of the position that he or she has assumed. Usually, this new principal has been given a charge to achieve some educational standard, such as raising test scores, improving attendance, or meeting the needs of special groups of students. But in working toward these important goals, the principal finds that there is also a host of related areas that must be considered and tended to. Teacher morale and proficiency are always related to school improvement. Money would facilitate many aspects of most programs, but dollars are often scarce. Parents and the rest of the school community must accept and support the school program if it is to succeed. And the principal must operate within the law.

Of all these program-related areas, new principals usually worry most about how they can operate within the host of legal and regulatory parameters that bound the operation of the school and dictate how things must be done. Perhaps this is because these legal parameters are seen to be the least forgiving. A gaffe with the faculty, while not a desirable occurrence, can be corrected by future actions. A misleading letter to parents, while damaging, can be corrected. Even an overspent budget will probably only bring a minor reprimand. But principals sense that a violation of the law, even one that occurs innocently and without apparent educational implications, may have severe consequences. Good common sense and knowledge of schools seem like a fairly adequate basis for staying out of trouble in staff relations, parent communications, and delivery of instruction. To the new principal, legal requirements often seem to be less the products of common sense.

Nor is the situation much improved for the experienced principal, even one who has been in the same position for many years. As David Sperry explains in this volume, legal and regulatory requirements are different in different states and localities, and, even in a single location, they change over time. Sperry notes in his first chapter that the knowledge base is both enormous and changing.

Accordingly, this text makes no attempt to provide a definitive knowledge base for the domain it describes. Instead, Sperry gives to the reader the principles, embodied in underlying values and concepts, that will provide the basis for understanding the knowledge base of the domain, for finding answers to specific questions about legal issues, and for enabling a proactive, preventative stance toward managing the legal and regulatory environment of the school.

This book is somewhat unique among books on law for school administrators. The purpose of the book is not to "teach the law" to the principal but to enable the principal to understand and use the law. Because the legal and regulatory dimensions in which schools must operate are constantly growing and shifting, it is clearly more important to develop a mode for growing in legal knowledge and using that knowledge to support the mission of the school than it is to master the content of a body of law. This text provides models and strategies for accomplishing these purposes of the book. Flow charts are used to illustrate how these strategies may be implemented. In effect, what this volume attempts to do is to equip the principal with a common sense about legal issues that puts it on a par with other domains where common sense seems to come more naturally.

This volume adds an important dimension to the *School Leadership Library*. The principal will find that every other domain is positively affected by an orientation to the law that recognizes it as a tool for providing stability and order, rather than a mechanism for ensuring perfunctory compliance. Once the principal assumes this orientation, the legal and regulatory environment will provide a supportive background for moving the school forward to the accomplishment of its mission.

David A. Erlandson
Alfred P. Wilson

ABOUT THE AUTHOR

Dr. David J. Sperry currently serves as professor and chair of the Department of Educational Leadership and Policy at the University of Utah. He is the lead coauthor of *Education Law and the Public Schools: A Compendium,* as well as the author of numerous other articles, books, and presentations largely dealing with school law and policy issues related to administrative practice in public education. Dr. Sperry has served on the Executive Committees of both the University Council for Educational Administration and the National Council for Professors of Educational Administration. He is a member of the Education Law Association. Dr. Sperry has taught in the public schools, served as an Associate Dean of Graduate School of Education at the University of Utah, and as an administrator with the Academic Affairs Office of the Utah System of Higher Education.

TABLE OF CONTENTS

1

INTRODUCING
EDUCATION LAW

Educational law is a fundamental and critical dimension of the knowledge base possessed by effective and successful school principals. As noted by the National Policy Board for Educational Administration (NPBEA), "Principals require a knowledge of legal and regulatory applications in order to address a range of complex and sensitive problems that arise in the school setting" (Thompson, 1993, p. 19-3). As further noted by the NPBEA, "Operating within the constraints of our system of laws and in accordance with its mandates requires both technical knowledge and awareness of the fundamental values that undergird legal and regulatory standards" (Thompson, 1993, p. 19-3). Legal decision-making skills are also necessary. Such skills include the ability to effectively gather facts, engage in the legal reasoning process, assess the current context in light of applicable law, formulate alternative courses of action, choose a plan of action, and implement the decision.

The NPBEA has also declared that:

> The costs of litigation, monetary and otherwise, require principals to adopt a preventative law ap-

proach to professional practice. "Knowledge of legal issues and competence in managing school risk are essential to avoid legal liability and to provide effective on-site leadership" (referencing Strahan & Turner, 1987). With this knowledge, principals can identify legal issues, foresee potential legal liability, and act to reduce or mitigate risks (Thompson, 1993, p. 19-4).

The legal and regulatory knowledge base critical to a principal's professional practice is, as noted by the NPBEA, a knowledge that "defines the scope of the principal's authority by identifying constraints and specifying the instrumentality for exercising power" (Thompson, 1993, p. 19-7). This particular knowledge base is enormous and emanates from all three branches of government (legislative, administrative, and judicial) at both the state and federal level, as well as from quasi-governmental bodies such as local boards of education. Unlike most of the other 20 domains which the National Policy Board has identified as critical to a principal's success, it is impossible to isolate a set of core learnings or standards from the knowledge base per se that would constitute a set of "best practices" or "uniform regulations" to which all school principals should adhere. This is true because of the enormity of the knowledge base and because only those school principals operating within the same school district would have the same exact set of regulatory and legal constraints. The only legal and regulatory applications that are common to all American school principals are those that originate from decisions of the United States Supreme Court, from laws and regulations enacted by Congress, and from regulations promulgated by the executive branch of the federal government. These common legal and regulatory applications only form a partial aggregate of the existing educational law knowledge base. Even with respect to these sources of educational law, local interpretations and practices may legitimately differ. Also, unlike some other domains where common standards or "best practices" might be said to be time honored, the legal and regulatory arena is one characterized by continual change, alteration, and refinement. In effect, the knowledge base is changing on a daily basis. Accordingly, no claim or effort is made in this book to present the actual knowledge base. Rather, the focus or purpose of the book is to present information, concepts, skills, and ideas that will enable a school principal to work more comfortably and effectively in a legal and regulatory environment.

Chapter 2 describes the primary sources and nature of the knowledge base, where the knowledge base is to be found, and how to access it. The chapter concludes by offering some practical suggestions for remaining current with respect to the knowledge base. Chapter 3 presents four key underlying values or concepts that ought to guide the thinking and actions of all public school principals committed to the professional and preventative management of the legal and regulatory dimensions of the school: (1) behaving in a reasonable manner; (2) according due process of law; (3) assuring equal protection of the law; and (4) respecting individual rights and freedoms. Chapter 4 presents an operational model of legal decision-making. This model offers a professional and defensible approach or framework for explicating the issues confronting school principals in the legal and regulatory domain. Chapter 5 introduces, in the form of legal decision-making flow charts, a succinct way in which principals can more effectively keep track of and utilize court decisions in their decision making and school management activities. The charts found in Chapter 5 are based on selected decisions of the United States Supreme Court and have been chosen for their applicability to everyday school level problems. Chapter 6 concludes the book by offering a variety of ideas and suggestions in the form of model policies, practices, and techniques designed to minimize legal liability and to foster a more preventative administrative approach to working in a legal and regulatory environment. These ideas and suggestions have been gathered from effective practicing school administrators, attorneys, risk management directors, professional organizations, and *West's Education Law Reporter*.

REFERENCES

Strahan, R.D., and L.C. Turner. (1987). *The Courts and the Schools*. White Plains, NY: Longman.

Thomson, S.D. (1993). *Principals for Our Changing Schools. The Knowledge and Skill Base.* Fairfax, VA: National Policy Board for Educational Administration.

2

THE SOURCES AND NATURE OF EDUCATIONAL LAW: UNDERSTANDING AND ACCESSING THE KNOWLEDGE BASE

WHAT IS EDUCATIONAL LAW?

The authority for the establishment and control of American public education is grounded in law. Therefore, the question naturally arises as to what is law and, more particularly, what is educational law? The United States Supreme Court wrote, "Law, in its generic sense, is a body of rules of action or conduct prescribed by controlling authority, and having binding legal force" (*Fidelity and Guaranty Co. v. Guenther*, 1930, p. 37). Hudgins and Vacca (1991, p. 2) define law as "a body of principles, standards, and rules that govern human behavior by creating obligations as well as rights, and by imposing penalties."

Because educational law pertains only to educational matters, it might be said that educational law is that portion of the larger body of law that establishes and controls the operation and management of schools, school systems, and other educational institutions and programs. Consistent with this definition, Alexander and Alexander (1992, p. 1) concluded that

> school law as a field of study is a generic term covering a wide range of legal subject matter including the basic fields of contracts, property, torts, constitutional law, and other areas of law that directly affect the educational and administrative processes of the educational system.

WHAT ARE THE SOURCES OF EDUCATIONAL LAW?

All primary law in the United States originates from four sources:

- constitutions
- statutes
- administrative rules and regulations
- court or case law

Elements of educational law in the United States emanate from all four sources.

CONSTITUTIONS

Constitutions are a body of precepts that provides a framework of law within which orderly governmental processes may operate. The United States Constitution does not provide a framework for public education; no specific mention of education is found in the federal Constitution. However, the Constitution's Tenth Amendment declares: "The powers not delegated to the United States by the Constitution, nor prohibited by it to the States are reserved to the States respectively, or to the people" (US Const, Amend X).

By virtue of this amendment, the responsibility for creating an organizational framework for public education is left to the individual states. All state constitutions provide for a system of public education. Although there is an amazing degree of similarity among the 50 educational systems, there are significant differences found in the constitutional language that creates them. Although each state constitution provides for the establishment of a public education system, some provide detailed direction regarding the organization, governance, and control of the system. Some even prescribe portions of the actual program and curriculum.

As stated earlier, the United States Constitution doesn't create a national system of education or give Congress authority to affirmatively direct and alter the educational mandates and policies of the individual states. The Constitution does, however, have a major impact on the governance and control of the individual state systems of education. Federal constitutional involvement comes about in several ways. The two most prominent are through the General Welfare Clause and the Fourteenth Amendment. The General Welfare Clause enables Congress to induce states to enact educational programs deemed important to the national welfare by providing federal tax dollars to support the creation and/or continuation of such programs. These incentives are often accompanied by certain requirements and restrictions that form very specific controls over the organization and management of the school system. The Fourteenth Amendment protects personal liberties against state intrusion. The applicable portion of the amendment reads:

> No state shall make or enforce any law which shall abridge the privileges or immunities of citizens of the United States; nor shall any State deprive any person of life, liberty, or property, without due process of law; nor deny to any person within its jurisdiction the equal protection of the laws (US Const, Amend XIV).

This amendment has been pivotal in many of the most significant judicial cases involving public education, including such diverse issues as racial discrimination, school finance, student discipline, and employment dismissal actions.

Although less obvious, other provisions of the Constitution do impact the operation and management of public school systems. For example, Article I, § 10 prohibits states from passing any law impairing the obligation of contracts. Public school districts regularly enter into contracts with employees and vendors. Any unilateral effort on the part of district officials or state legislators to alter such contracts, particularly in a detrimental or harmful manner, would violate this constitutional prohibition. Another example is Article I, § 8, which grants Congress power to regulate commerce including commerce among the several states. This provision affects schools largely through statutes and regulations governing transportation, safety, and labor (e.g., minimum wage laws and school bus standards).

STATUTES

By definition, statutes are acts of the legislative branch of government that declare, command, or prohibit something. In some jurisdictions, statutes may be enacted by or through a vote of the electorate. Statutory law is sometimes referred to as the written law.

The United States Congress is limited in its statutory power to that which the federal Constitution permits. Accordingly, its efforts to impact or affect public education in the United States must come about largely through indirect means. While the federal government operates with limited powers in this domain, state legislatures generally have broad authority to control and manage their respective public education systems. Except for Hawaii, all state legislative bodies have delegated the day-to-day management of public schools to local administrative units, which are most commonly called boards of education (Hawaii has a single statewide board). As noted by an Ohio court:

> Boards of education are...creatures of statute and their duties as well as their authority are clearly defined by the state legislation on the subject. Their authority or jurisdiction is derived solely from statute and is limited strictly to such powers as are

clearly and expressly granted to them or are clearly implied and necessary for the execution of the powers expressly granted. They have special powers which are to be strictly construed, and which they cannot exceed; and since the boards of education have only such authority as is conferred by law, when they take action outside of and against the plain provisions of the law, such action is absolutely void (*Stanley v. Luke*, 1962, p. 701).

Except for constitutional limitations, the state legislature may enlarge or abridge the authority of school boards as it sees fit. (See *Love v. City of Dallas*, 1931).

ADMINISTRATIVE RULES AND REGULATIONS

Administrative rules and regulations are promulgated by executive agencies of government as directed by legislative bodies to carry out statutory provisions. This form of law is usually referred to as administrative law. At the federal level, administrative rules and regulations ordinarily take one of two forms: either rules and regulations issued by cabinet-level departments and other federal agencies, or executive orders issued by the president of the United States. At the state level, the process works in a similar fashion with either state agencies issuing rules and regulations designed to carry out the directives of the legislature or the governor issuing executive orders. Other administrative rules and regulations in a public school context are those policies and regulations adopted by local boards of education. It should also be noted that administrative decision-making by superintendents and school principals is a rule having force of law. At the lowest level, even an impromptu decision by a school employee is considered a rule.

CASE LAW

Rules of law enunciated by the courts are referred to as case law. Much of the study of law is focused on case law because of the unique role the courts play. Courts have three basic tasks. First, is the responsibility to determine the constitutionality of legislative or administrative action. For example, if a local school board authorizes its high schools to include a christian hymn as part of its graduation exercise and someone complains that such an authorization is in violation of the First Amendment of the United States Constitution, the courts become the final arbitrator of the dispute by determining whether or not the practice is in accord with or in violation of the Constitution. Second, courts construe or interpret legislative enactments. For example, a state statute may require that all school personnel be entitled to remediation before dismissal. The language of the statute, however, may fail to provide sufficient or adequate answers to critical questions such as whether or not all grounds for dismissal for alleged misbehavior are remediable or what constitutes adequate remediation. Courts are empowered to give answers to these questions by rendering an interpretation of what they consider to have been the legislative intent and meaning. In so doing, courts will generally trace the legislative history and debate surrounding the original passage of the statute. Finally, courts settle controversies by applying principles of law to specific sets of facts. For example, in personal injury cases involving the schools, courts are often called on to determine whether a given injury was due to the negligence of a school employee. By applying the principles of law governing negligence, a court is able to make a determination and render a decision.

It is important to an understanding of case law to realize that courts don't act on their own initiative. They assume jurisdiction only of those controversies and other legal matters referred to them. Thus, it is possible for a school official(s) to be administering a school or program which in some manner is in violation of a constitutional, statutory, or regulatory requirement. Yet, unless the act, method, or practice is challenged in a court of law, it could go unaltered for a long time. For example, many public schools in the United States were racially segregated until 1954 when the practice was legally challenged as violating the Fourteenth Amendment's Equal Protection Clause. This argument was sustained by the United States Supreme Court (see *Brown v. Board of Education of Topeka*, 1954).

A second important aspect of case law that needs to be understood is that a court will only decide the fact situation before it. Seldom, if ever, are the factual situations in two cases identical. Changes in such matters as time, place, individual(s) involved, technology, knowledge, public values, scientific advancements, sponsorship, or organizational structure, often lead to a significant difference in case outcomes. For example, in 1948, the legality of providing a voluntary religious instructional program in the public schools was found unconstitutional by the United States Supreme Court *(People ex rel. McCollum v. Board of Education*, 1948). Four years later, the Supreme Court upheld a religious instructional program. Rather than the program being sponsored by the school and taught in a public school building, it was offered privately by the churches in the community and taught in off-campus facilities. Students who desired to participate were granted released time from the public schools to attend the religious classes (see *Zorach v. Clauson*, 1952). In this instance, changes in time, place, and sponsorship altered the facts sufficiently to justify a different judicial outcome.

This concept speaks to the dynamic nature of the law. Although courts strive for a measure of consistency in the law through the doctrine of *stare decisis* (to stand by decided cases) and the rule of precedent (once a point of law has been determined by the courts, it is fixed law and can be changed only by competent authority), the great myth of the law is that the law is certain, exact, and fixed. The law is not stationary; it is continually evolving as courts reinterpret constitutional and statutory provisions and legislatures enact new laws. This is why best practices in educational law should not be based solely on knowledge of a specific statute, administrative regulation, or court case, but rather on an understanding of the lawmaking process.

Finally, it is important to understand how the court systems function in the United States. The federal court system has three tiers: the United States Supreme Court at the top; the United States Courts of Appeals—an intermediate appellate court divided into regional circuits and a few specialized courts; and District Courts—trial courts found in each state. Decisions of the Supreme Court are good law for the entire

country and must be followed everywhere. Decisions of the
Courts of Appeals and District Courts, however, are binding
only within their geographical jurisdiction.

State court systems are similarly organized into appeals
courts and trial courts although the names selected for these
courts vary by state. Most states have a supreme court (the
highest court of appeals in the state), an intermediate appellate court or system of courts, and a system of trial courts.
Court decisions of the highest court of a state establish the
legal standards only for the state within which the court is located. Lower state court decisions also are binding only within the jurisdiction of the court. State court jurisdictions, unlike some federal court jurisdictions, do not cross state lines.

WHAT IS THE RELATIONSHIP BETWEEN AND AMONG THE VARIOUS SOURCES OF EDUCATIONAL LAW?

Because educational law emanates from multiple sources,
it is important to understand the relationship between and
among these sources. The following explanation and accompanying Table 2.1 (found on pages 14–15), developed by
Charles F. Faber and Thomas Diamantes (1996, pp. 1-3–1-5),
provide a clear and succinct answer to understanding these
relationships.

HIERARCHY OF SCHOOL LAW

Because there are different types of law, emanating
from various sources, the effective operation of our
legal system depends upon the existence of a
clear-cut hierarchy of law. If two laws are in conflict, it is essential to know which law prevails.

As the Constitution of the United States is the
basic framework upon which the structure of government is constructed, it is the supreme law of the
land. It is superior to the constitutional provisions
of each of the states, superior to Congressional and
state legislative enactments, and superior to all

kinds of administrative law. In order to be valid, all other law must be in accord with the Constitution.

At the national level the Constitution is supreme, then, followed in hierarchical order by statutory law, and finally by administrative law. Case law is interpretative law and its place in the hierarchy depends on the kind of law being interpreted. The rank order is always: first, constitutional; second, statutory; third, administrative.

Law can be changed only by competent authority; that is, by the agency that made the law or by a higher authority. The Constitution as ratified by the several states can be changed only by following the amendment process specified in the document itself. Of course, interpretation of the Constitution, that is, deciding what it means in a particular case, may be changed by the appropriate competent authority—the courts. The Supreme Court is the highest court, and all other courts are bound by its decisions. Through the doctrine of *stare decisis...* and the rule of precedent it...is fixed law and can be changed only by competent authority. Although the Supreme Court almost always follows precedent, it can overrule a previous decision. It seldom does this, but when it does so it does it explicitly and with a careful statement of reasons for overruling the previous decision or for declaring why the precedent does not apply to the case under consideration. Thus, case law can and does change.

All statutes enacted by the United States Congress must be in accord with the Constitution and are subject by the Supreme Court to see that they meet that criterion (if challenged by someone who claims to be damaged by a particular statute) and are also subject to interpretation by the courts.

Except for certain presidential powers assigned by the Constitution, all administrative law promulgated by the executive branch must not only be
in accord with the Constitution but also must have

TABLE 2.1. HIERARCHY AND SOURCE OF SCHOOL LAW

Level	Constitutional	Statutory
National	**1A** Source: Constitution of the United States Priority: Top Subject to interpretation by 1D	**1B** Source: U.S. Congress Priority: Second only to 1A Subject to interpretation by 1D
State	**2A** Source: State constitution Priority: As state law, top (but cannot conflict with 1A) Subject to interpretation by 2D and (if a federal question is involved) by 1D	**2B** Source: State legislature Priority: As state law, second to 2A Subject to interpretation by 2D and (if a federal question is involved) by 1D
Local	**3A** None	**3B** Quasi-statutory only Source: School board Priority: Behind all applicable laws at levels 1 and 2 Subject to interpretation by 2D and (if a federal question is involved) by 1D

The thick lines indicate the separation of powers between the legislative, executive, and judicial branches, and the division of powers between the national and state levels.

Administrative	*Case*
1C Source: Executive branch and administrative agencies of United States Priority: Third, behind 1A and 1B Subject to interpretation by 1D	**1D** Source: Supreme Court of the United States and other federal courts
2C Source: Executive branch and administrative agencies of the state Priority: As state law, third to 2A and 2B. If legitimate federal interest intervenes, it is also behind 1B and 1C Subject to interpretation by 2D and (if a federal question is involved) by 1D	**2D** Source: State Supreme Court and other state courts (if a federal question is involved, must not conflict with 1D)
3C Source: School board, superintendent, and other administrators Priority: Lowest Subject to interpretation by 3B, 2C, and 2D and (if a federal question is involved) by 1D	**3D** No true judicial power at local school district level

The thin lines represent the lack of separation of power
at the local level and the lack of division of power
between the state and local level.

statutory authorization. In other words, rules and regulations issued by the Department of Education can be valid only if they are conceived in order to implement some program authorized by Congress. In regard to such rules and regulations, the function of the courts is threefold—to see that they do not violate the Constitution, to see that they do not exceed Congressional authorization or subvert Congressional intent, and to interpret the meaning of the rules in specific questions. All of these duties arise only when brought to the court in a justifiable controversy by an appropriate party.

At the state level, a somewhat similar hierarchy prevails. The state constitution, provided it does not conflict with the Constitution of the United States, is supreme. Statutes enacted by the state legislature need to be in accord with both constitutions. Rules and regulations of state administrative agencies must be constitutional and in line with statutory requirements. State courts are bound to recognize the supremacy of the Constitution of the United States and (in the absence of conflicts) of the state constitution and to recognize the authority of statutory law enacted by the state legislature over administrative law. State courts must recognize the supremacy of federal courts in dealing with federal questions. There is a hierarchy of courts within each state to handle state cases.

At the local level the situation is quite different. Local school districts are not recognized by the U.S. Constitution and are recognized to a very limited degree, if at all, by state constitutions. There is no equivalent of a constitution at the local level. There is even no real local equivalent of a legislative body. The local school board is a quasi-legislative, quasi-administrative agency. Its policies are law, only in a very limited sense. A school board cannot enact criminal law, and its civil law authority is very rigidly restricted by the state legislature. The division of responsibility between a school board and its administrative staff is nowhere near as clear-cut as that between Congress and the President, for example. Unless this division is specified by state statutes, it is likely to be very fuzzy indeed. Furthermore, there is nothing remotely approaching a court to make case law at the local school district level. The board of education itself is the hearing agency in student expulsion cases, for example. Thus, the board serves not only in a quasi-legislative and quasi-administrative, but in a quasi-judicial capacity as well.

WHERE IS THE EDUCATIONAL LAW KNOWLEDGE BASE TO BE FOUND AND HOW DOES ONE ACCESS IT?

The primary sources of educational law are found in both printed and electronic formats (the latter format is discussed separately at the end of this section). The location of the officially published version of each form of primary law is noted in Table 2.2 on page 18. It should be apparent to even the most casual observer of the table, that trying to collect copies of all the applicable laws, regulations, cases, and constitutional items comprising the educational laws governing public education in the United States, would constitute a major undertaking and would result in a collection of an immense amount of material. Although a compilation of rules and regulations of the thousands of local school districts throughout the United States has never been assembled, most major law school libraries and some large government document libraries house copies of the federal and state codes, state administrative rules and regulations, and case books or reporters that contain the appellate level decisions and opinions of federal and state courts. Large public libraries also house many of these publications.

Codes, particularly state codes, are familiar to most public school principals. They contain constitutional and statutory material and are printed in multivolume compilations

TABLE 2.2. LOCATION OF PRIMARY EDUCATIONAL LAW SOURCES

Level	Constitutional	Statutory	Administrative	Case	
National	Source: United States Code	Source: United States Code	Source: Code of Federal Regulations	Court: United States Supreme Court United States Courts of Appeals United States District Courts	Sources: United States Reports Federal Reporter Federal Supplement
Source	Source: Constitution volume of the state code	Source: State codes	Source: State administrative rules and regulations (titles vary by state)	Court: State appellate courts	Sources: State reporter or one of the West's regional reporters
Local	Not applicable	Not applicable	Source: Policies, rules, and regulations adopted by local boards of education	Not applicable	

organized by subject matter. Every state, as well as the federal government, annually publishes a new version of its code or a cumulative supplement to its existing code. At the federal level, every new law is initially published separately in the form of a *slip law*. Copies of slip laws are found at a number of locations and in a number of publications. All 1,400 libraries designated as depositories for United States government publications receive copies of these slip laws as do other libraries that subscribe to these publications. They are also found in the *United States Code Congressional and Administrative News, United States Law Week,* and *United States Code Service Advance Service.*

At the end of each session of Congress, all slip laws are compiled and published in the *United States Statutes at Large.* Every six years, all federal laws still in force are compiled into what is called the *United States Code.* Supplements are published during the intervening years. Annotated versions of the code are published by private companies. West Publishing Company publishes the *United States Code Annotated* (U.S.C.A.) and Lawyers Cooperative Publishing Company prints the *United States Code Service* (U.S.C.S.).

States follow a similar format although not all states publish separate volumes for each legislative session. Those states that do publish such compilations call them session laws. Most codes contain a separate index volume to help find the topic being researched.

Administrative rules and regulations are also published in multivolumes and organized by subject matter. At the federal level, as new administrative rules and regulations and executive orders are formulated they are published daily (except on official federal holidays, Saturdays, and Sundays) in the *Federal Register.* All regulations in force are regularly codified in the *Code of Federal Regulations,* which is published annually in quarterly installments. At the state level, some states produce a compilation of all state regulations, while in other states the rules and regulations are published separately by each state agency.

Court opinions are found, as noted in Table 2.2, in court reporters. Reporters are sequentially numbered bound volumes that contain court opinions arranged chronologically.

The official opinions of the United States Supreme Court are found in the *United States Reports*. They are also found in numerous electronic formats and in these bound volumes: *West's Supreme Court Reporter; United States Supreme Court Reports, Lawyers' Edition; United States Law Week;* and *United States Supreme Court Bulletin.* The opinions of the United States Courts of Appeal are found in the *Federal Reporter* and federal District Court opinions are contained in the *Federal Supplement.* State opinions are found in either or both state reporters or West's regional reporters. Reference to court opinions is by citation. A citation consists of the volume number, the abbreviation of the reporter, and the page number where the opinion begins. For example, the United States Supreme Court opinion in *Tinker v. Des Moines Independent Community School District* is found at 393 U.S. 503. The volume number is 393; the reporter containing the opinion is the *United States Reports*, and the opinion begins on page 503.

Locating statutory and regulatory materials is relatively easy because these forms of primary law are published and organized by subject matter, kept up to date through cumulative supplements or new editions that are comprised of only those laws that are in force, and are generally accompanied by an alphabetical subject index. Searching for material found in court opinions is not as easy because cases aren't organized by subject matter nor discarded when no longer "good law." Accordingly, the legal researcher needs to become familiar with two very important finding tools. The first is the American Digest System. This is a system which takes each published court opinion and writes a summary paragraph of the points of law in the case. These paragraphs are then organized by topic into multivolume digests, which permits the researcher access to court opinions by subject matter.

The second finding tool is a citator. Citators, as noted by Jacobstein, Mersky, and Dunn (1994, p. 286), are "sources, available in print and electronic format, that provide, through letter-form abbreviations or words, the subsequent history and interpretation of reported cases, and list the cases and legislative enactments construing, applying, or affecting statutes." In effect, citators allow the researcher to determine whether or not the case being researched or cited contains law that can be relied on.

There are many secondary sources that can also be valuable to the researcher in finding primary law sources, including such things as legal encyclopedias, looseleaf services, journals, and legal treatises. It is beyond the purpose and scope of this book to identify and describe each one. Nevertheless, obtaining the necessary skills to effectively utilize primary legal documents, to make use of law libraries, and to conduct basic legal research is not overwhelming; many school principals and other educational leaders have acquired reasonable proficiency in doing so. Principals wishing to develop these kinds of skills should probably take a course on legal research or consult one of several books available on how to conduct legal research, such as *Legal Research Illustrated* by Jacobstein, Mersky, and Dunn. Now in its sixth edition, the book offers graphic illustrations that make the research process easy to understand and follow. The book is published by The Foundation Press, Inc., Westbury, New York. Educational law courses offered in universities where law libraries exist generally provide students with an introduction to using law libraries and to conducting legal research. (Caution: It is always a good idea for principals to review the results of their research with a competent attorney, especially if there is any doubt or concern as to the potential outcome(s) or consequence(s) of using such information.)

Most primary and secondary legal sources are also available in a variety of electronic formats including computer-assisted legal research systems, CD-ROM libraries, and on the Internet. The technological developments that have made this form of legal research possible have largely come about over the last two decades. As a result, legal research is more convenient and accessible to a greater number of individuals, including more school principals and other school officials. It does, however, require access to a personal computer.

LEXIS and WESTLAW are the two major legal computer research systems. The companies that have developed these systems will, for a fee, provide the researcher with access to virtually all primary legal documents and most secondary legal sources through a telecommunications system. Most of their legal libraries are also available, for a fee, on CD-ROMS. The addresses, telephone numbers, and Internet addresses for contacting these companies are:

LEXIS Law Publishing   West Group
The Michie Company   610 Opperman Drive
PO Box 7587   St. Paul, Minnesota 55123
Charlottesville, Virginia 22907   1-800-255-2549
www.lexis.com   www.westgroup.com

A number of other commercial companies provide various legal databases on CD-ROM. One of the better known companies that publishes both an Education Law and a Special Education Law CD-ROM is LRP Publications:

LRP Publications
747 Dresher Road (Dept. 425)
Horsham, Pennsylvania 19044-0980
1-800-341 7874 ext. 245
www.lrp.com

In addition to the abovementioned telecommunications and CD-ROM systems, there has been a growing number of both fee-based and free sites on the Internet that provide access to primary and secondary legal materials. Use caution, however, when utilizing these sites. Anyone can publish on the Web. To help evaluate the information found, look for the following:

- ♦ Author—the person or organization responsible for compiling the Web page.
- ♦ Publication Date—the date the Web page was created.
- ♦ Revision Date—the date the Web page was last revised.
- ♦ Citations—references and sources from which the material is taken.
- ♦ URL Address—the Web page address has a naming convention that tells what kind of information is on the page. If it ends with:

- .org (organization)—Attempts to influence public opinion; these pages are usually sponsored by some type of advocacy group.
- .com (commercial)—Tries to sell or promote products; these pages are usually sponsored by some type of commercial enterprise. Also, news agencies use this domain extension.
- .edu (education)—Educational institutions present factual information on these pages.
- .gov (government)—Government agencies present factual information on these pages.

Miner and Thomas (1998) consider the following to be among the most reliable and useful sites currently available for accessing primary and secondary legal materials over the Internet:

PRIMARY SOURCES

Federal Legal Information

Cases

U.S. Supreme Court	**http://supct.law.cornell.edu./supct/** [1990 to present, key word searchable] **http://www.fedworld.gov/supcourt/inex.htm** [1937–1975, covers vols. 300–422 of US Reports; includes 325 selected historic decisions, some pre-1937] **http://www.law.vill.edu/Fed-Ct/sct.html** [Access using U.S. Report volume, key word searchable]
U.S. Law Week	**http://subscript.bna.com** [fee-based service]

Courts of Appeal   **http://www.law.emory.edu/FEDCTS**
                    [All circuit court of appeals decisions are
                        located at this site. Date coverage var-
                        ies. Key word searchable.]

                    **http://www.versuslaw.com (fee-based
                        service)**
                    [Some Circuit Courts of Appeal decisions
                        back to 1930]

District Courts   **http://www.law.vill.edu/Fed-Ct/
                        fedcourt.html**
                    [Contains opinions from the following
                        courts: District of Columbia, Florida
                        Southern District, New Mexico, Texas
                        Southern District, Kansas Bankruptcy
                        Court, New Mexico Bankruptcy Court,
                        Idaho Bankruptcy Court, Massachu-
                        setts Bankruptcy Court, and Virginia
                        Bankruptcy Court, Eastern District.
                        Date coverage varies.]

Statutes & Bills

United States   **http://www.law.cornell.edu/uscode/**
    Code   [Key word searchable] [not current]

U.S. Constitution   **http://info.rutgers.edu/Library/Refer-
                        ence/US/constitution/**

Bills   **http://thomas.loc.gov**
                    [Key word searchable] [also includes re-
                        cent committee reports, congressional
                        record]

Regulations

Code of Federal   **http://law.house.gov/4.htm**
    Regulations   [Key word searchable]

Federal Register   **http://www.gpo.ucop.edu/**
                    [Key word searchable. From 1995 to
                        today]

Federal Agencies

Federal Agencies   **http://www.law.vill.edu/fed-agency/
                     fedwebloc.html**
                     [Links to federal agencies on the Web]

Other Web Sites

GPO Access Sites   At the Government Printing Office Access sites you will have access to the United States Code, Congressional Bills, Congressional Calendars, Congressional Documents, Congressional Record and Index, Congressional Reports, History of Bills and Resolutions, Federal Register, GAO Reports and Decisions and Public Laws (and more is being added all the time).

http://www.gpo.ucop.edu (good template for federal register searches)
http://thorplus.lib.purdue.edu:8100/gpo/
http://mel.lib.mi.us/gpo/
**http://www.access.gpo.gov/su_docs/
aces/aaces002.html**
http://sailor.lib.md.us/forms/gpo.html

Recent Federal   **http://www.courts.com/appoint.htm**
Court Ap-
pointments

White House   **http://www.whitehouse.gov**

U.S. House of   **http://law.house.gov**
Representatives

Oral Argument   **http://oyez.nwu.edu/**
Archive   [Provides information about major constitutional cases heard and decided by the U.S. Supreme Court. Audio files begin in 1995 and are downloadable.]

| Directory of Electronic Public Access Services to Automated Information in the U.S. Federal Courts | **http://www.uscourts.gov/PubAccess.html** |

All States Legal Information

WashLaw	**http://lawlib.wuacc.edu/washlaw/uslaw/statelaw.html** [All 50 states are listed. Select one and a list of the legal materials available on the Internet for that state is listed, along with the Internet addresses. Just click and you are there! Note: sites are always changing so some links may not work.]
VersusLaw	**http://www.versuslaw.com** (fee-based service) [Appellate court cases from all 50 states; many back to 1930.]
LOIS	**http://www.pita.com** (fee-based service) [Cases, statutes, regulations, and attorney general opinions for over 20 states with more states being added regularly.]
City & County Codes	**http://www.spl.org/govpubs/municode.html** [Selected city and county codes from over 43 states around the country]
State & Local Government Pages	**http://www.piperinfo.com/state/states.html**

SECONDARY SOURCES

Reference Aids

Bibliographic Formats for Citing electronic Information	**http://www.uvm.edu/~ncrane/estyles**
Dictionary and Thesaurus	**http://www.dictionary.com**
Forms	**http://www.findlaw.com/16forms/ index.html**
	http://www.lectlaw.com/form.html
	http://lawlib.wuacc.edu/washlaw/ legalforms/legalforms.html
	[These sites provide access to a variety of legal and business forms.]
Legal Dictionary	**http://www.islandnet.com/~wwlia/ diction.htm**

Journal Articles

Electronic Journals	**http://www.awreview.org/**
Legal and Law Related Journals	**http://www.usc.edu/dept/law-lib/ legal/journals.html**
Tables of Contents of over 750 Law Reviews	**http://tarlton.law.utexas.edu/tallons/ content_search.html**

HOW DOES ONE OBTAIN A MINIMAL WORKING UNDERSTANDING OF THE EDUCATIONAL LAW KNOWLEDGE BASE?

Given the multiple tasks and skills required of modern day school principals, there is a limit to the time that school principals can devote to becoming acquainted with the educational law knowledge base. For the average school principal, however, at least three tasks should be undertaken to gain a minimal working understanding of this particular knowledge base:

- *Complete an introductory university-level course on educational law.* Most states require a course in educational law as a prerequisite for obtaining certification as a school administrator. Such courses typically use one or more of the many excellent general treatises, casebooks, compendiums, and other materials that have been developed over the past several decades. Although not to be viewed as a source of primary law, these secondary educational law resources offer the reader a summary of the critical topics, cases, statutes, rules, regulations, and current developments in the law that affect the management and control of public schools. Most of these books present a national rather than local perspective of the law. Nevertheless, a good course will provide principals with a general familiarity of this important dimension of the knowledge base. Furthermore, such courses can help principals become more sensitive to the range of potential legal problems they could face and provide help and suggestions on how to prevent or minimize legal problems within the schools.

- *Become acquainted with the state educational law code and state-level educational law rules and regulations of the state in which one is practicing.* Many states publish a document containing this information and even include copies of important state Attorney General Opinions regarding legal questions and issues about the control and management of the schools within the state. If not published as a separate document, this same material can be found in the state code and state administrative rules and regulations manual. Principals should keep an up-to-date copy of these documents in their personal or school libraries.

♦ *Become completely familiar with the rules and regulations of the board of education and the local school district within which one is working.* This familiarity includes not only the written policies and procedures but the unwritten practices of the district.

HOW DOES ONE REMAIN CURRENT WITH RESPECT TO THE EDUCATIONAL LAW KNOWLEDGE BASE?

In addition to those steps required to gain an initial understanding of the educational law knowledge base, principals should develop a plan for remaining current with the knowledge base because the educational law knowledge base is subject to constant change. This is one domain where school principals should seek constant in-service and professional development in order to keep skills and knowledge up-to-date. Some practical suggestions for keeping current are:

♦ *Remain familiar with the changes in policies and procedures of the board of education and school district within which one is employed.* New policies and regulations should be read carefully and filed appropriately. Attendance at district in-service or principal's meetings where these items are discussed and reviewed is critical.

♦ *Remain current with state-level actions of the legislature, state education agency, state courts, and other agencies, which involve educational, legal, and regulatory developments affecting the schools.* This can often be accomplished by reading newspapers, attending in-service meetings, participating in state-level educational law conferences, and by making sure that personal copies of the state code and state-level administrative rules and regulations manuals are kept up-to-date.

♦ *Remain sensitive to national developments as they pertain to new landmark court cases and federal statutory and regulatory actions involving schools.* There are several practical things a school principal can do to achieve this recommendation including:

- Maintain membership in and attend the annual convention of the Education Law Association (ELA), formerly the National Organization on Legal Problems of Education or (NOLPE). The ELA is a national organization consisting of school administrators, university professors, lawyers, and students. ELA's purpose is to improve education by promoting interest in and understanding of education law. Membership in the organization includes receipt of the monthly *School Law Reporter* newsletter, which provides timely information on new court cases and other developments in educational law. ELA also publishes an annual yearbook, *The Yearbook of School Law*, and a monograph series on educational law topics, both of which have everyday application to the administration of schools. The Education Law Association's address is 300 College Park, Dayton, Ohio 45469-2280.

- Subscribe to one or more of the excellent education law newsletters. In addition to the one provided by the ELA, several of the national associations to which many school administrators belong publish education law newsletters. An example is *A Legal Memorandum,* which is a monthly publication of the National Association of Secondary School Principals. There are also several well-done commercial educational law newsletters available.

- Attend state or national level educational law institutes or conferences. Conferences organized by or in some combination with state education agencies, university departments of educational administration, or state bar associations are offered in many states.

- Purchase an educational law looseleaf service such as *Education Law and the Public Schools: A Compendium,* which is published by Christopher-Gordon Publishers Inc., 1502 Providence Highway, Suite 12, Norwood, Massachusetts 02062. This particular publication provides easy access to over 100 common educational law topics and issues facing school administrators and offers practical suggestions to vexing educational law problems.

- Subscribe to one or more education law journals. Two prominent and well-known journals are the *Journal of Law and Education* and *West's Educational Law Reporter.* The *Journal of Law and Education* is jointly edited by the University of South Carolina Law School and the University of Louisville School of Law and is published by Jefferson Law Book Co., 2100 Huntington Ave., Baltimore, Maryland 21211. *West's Educational Law Reporter* is published by the West Publishing Co., 610 Opperman Drive, P.O. Box 64526, St. Paul, Minnesota 55164-0526.

Additional ideas and suggestions for gaining and maintaining a working understanding of the educational law knowledge base are found in Chapters 5 and 6.

REFERENCES

Alexander, K., and M.D. Alexander, (1998). *American Public School Law* (4th ed.). Belmont, CA: International Thomson Publishing Company.

Brown v. Board of Education of Topeka, 347 U.S. 483 (1954).

Faber, C.F., and T. Diamantes. (1996). *School Law for Kentucky Teachers and Administrators* (8th ed.). Crestview Hills, KY: Rhinegold Publishing.

Fidelity and Guaranty Co. v. Guenther, 281 U.S. 34 (1930).

Hudgins, H.C. Jr., and R.S. Vacca. (1991). *Law and Education: Contemporary Issues and Court Decisions* (3rd ed.). Charlottesville, VA: Michie Company.

Jacobstein, J.M., R.M. Mersky, and D.J. Dunn. (1994). *Legal Research Illustrated* (6th ed.). Westbury, NY: Foundation Press.

Love v. City of Dallas, 40 S.W.2d 20 (Tex. 1931).

Miner, S., and M. Thomas. (1998). *Legal Research on the Internet.* Salt Lake City: University of Utah S.J. Quinney Law Library.

People ex rel. McCollum v. Board of Education, 333 U.S. 203 (1948).

Stanley v. Like, 190 N.E.2d 697 (Ohio Com. Pl. 1962) (*quoting from* 48 Ohio Jur. 2d 481, 578).

Zorach v. Clauson, 343 U.S. 306 (1952).

3

EDUCATIONAL LAW: UNDERLYING VALUES AND CONCEPTS

VALUES AND CONCEPTS IDENTIFIED

The legal and regulatory environment in which American public school principals serve is based on important legal concepts and cultural values that must be both understood and carefully safeguarded. These values and concepts are reflected in America's basic documents such as the Declaration of Independence, the United States Constitution, and the state constitutions. The nation's cultural heritage also furnishes important legal concepts and practices. For example, a critical element of our governmental and regulatory arenas has been our acceptance and continued usage of the "common law." *Black's Law Dictionary* (1990, p. 276) defines the common law as

> ...the body of those principles and rules of action, relating to the government and security of persons and property, which derive their authority solely

from usages and customs of immemorial antiq-
uity, or from the judgments and decrees of the
courts recognizing, affirming, and enforcing such
usages and customs; and, in this sense, particularly
the ancient unwritten law of England. In general, it
is a body of law that develops and derives through
judicial decisions, as distinguished from legislative enactments.

Much of American tort law (a tort is a private or civil wrong
or injury, other than a breach of contract, for which courts will
provide a remedy in the form of monetary damages), for example, is derived from the common law.

An examination of these basic documents and legal tradi-
tions reveals a number of fundamental values and concepts.
Four that seem especially critical for the administration of
public schools are:

+ Behave in a fair and reasonable manner.
+ Accord due process of law.
+ Assure equal protection of the law.
+ Respect individual rights and freedoms.

It is purposeful that each value statement begins with an
action verb. It is intended to suggest that in addition to understanding the particular elements of the value or concept,
there is an affirmative professional and personal duty and responsibility to act or execute one's position and authority in
compliance and in harmony with the value or concept. As
one of America's most important and critical institutions, the
public schools have an obligation to foster and promote the
democratic values on which the legal and regulatory system
is based. Furthermore, it is arguable that school principals
ought to have or should develop an internal and personal
value system consistent with these statements. A lack of regard for and failure to give appropriate attention to such
principles may ultimately result in serious legal problems in
the school environment.

BEHAVING IN A FAIR AND
REASONABLE MANNER

The principles of "fairness and reasonableness" permeate the law. They are significant concepts and are often viewed synonymously. *Black's Law Dictionary* (1990, p. 595) defines "fair" as "having the qualities of impartiality and honesty; free from prejudice, favoritism, and self-interest; just; equitable; even-handed; equal as between conflicting interests." The dictionary defines "reasonable" as being "fair, proper, just, moderate, suitable under the circumstances. Fit and appropriate to the end in view....Not immoderate or excessive, being synonymous with rational, honest, equitable, fair, suitable, moderate, tolerable" (p. 1265).

These terms form the basis for many of the legal standards employed within the law as in, for example: fair and impartial jury; fair and impartial trial; fair comment; fair use doctrine; fair rate of return; reasonable cause; reasonable belief; reasonable care; reasonable doubt; reasonable force; reasonable grounds; reasonable notice; reasonable suspicion; and reasonable time.

The concepts also apply to the expected conduct and behavior of individuals. As noted by McCarthy, Bull, Quantz, and Sorenson (1994, pp. 1273–1274), "Educators and all citizens are expected to act reasonably in light of their experience and training. This means that school administrators are expected to act in the same manner as reasonable individuals with their educational backgrounds and certification under similar conditions." They also note that "actions that would be reasonable in one set of circumstances may be unreasonable in another situation" (p. 1274). This conduct and behavioral expectation relate to both the normal interaction and communication between and among individuals, and, in the school setting, the manner in which rules and regulations are established and enforced. In determining the reasonableness and fairness of a rule or action, one ordinarily looks for a valid objective (something within the power or authority of the individual to perform) and a rational means or connection for carrying out the objective. It is important to understand that the means need not (in most instances) be the most expeditious, popular, or least expensive; however, the means should be grounded in a rational, reasoned judgment based on such things as research, scientific evidence, established laws, and personal experience. For example, a principal might recommend to a school board that site A be selected over site B for the construction of a new school. It may not be the most popular choice with parents, and the recommended site might cost more money. However, demographic studies may demonstrate that within four to five years the population base will be better served by site A, or that future traffic patterns will make site A a safer location.

Personal behavior and rules promulgated by school officials will be viewed as unfair or unreasonable when they are brought about by arbitrary, capricious, wanton, or discriminatory reasons. Each term deserves defining.

- *Arbitrary* refers to conduct or acts based upon one's will and not upon any course of reasoning and exercise of judgment. Arbitrary acts are those not supported by solid and substantial cause and/or without reasons given.

- *Capricious* refers to conduct or acts based upon an abrupt change in feeling, opinion, or actions proceeding from some whim or fancy; irrational notion; or irresponsible inclination.

- *Wanton* refers to conduct or acts characterized by a reckless disregard of the rights and safety of others.

- *Discriminatory* refers to conduct or acts that provide unfair treatment or denial of normal privileges to persons because of such things as race, age, sex, nationality, or religion.

Despite the clear responsibility that school officials have to behave in a fair and reasonable manner, it must be understood that these concepts are not always precise, easily known, or universally accepted standards of behavior and performance. There is no foolproof test or system for determining whether particular conduct is fair or reasonable. Furthermore, these concepts are not static and unchanging. In making judgments about fairness and reasonableness, an administrator is, at best, approximating what is deemed acceptable and what is not. The ultimate determiner is a court of law. Courts generally use a legal fiction known as the "reasonable man" doctrine or standard in assessing the question. This legal yardstick ordinarily calls on a panel of one's peers (a jury) to answer this question: "What would a reasonable and prudent person have done under similar circumstances?" Or, in the case of a professionally licensed or certified individual, to answer this question: "What would a reasonable and prudent individual with like training and preparation have done under similar circumstances?" This is not a perfect system but represents the best we have. Different juries can, and on rare occasions do, vary in their answers to questions involving the exact same set of facts and circumstances put before them. This can be seen from time to time in cases where more than one person is injured in the same accident, but separate jury trials are brought for each injured party. Different outcomes in these cases can be attributed to the unique background, experience, and beliefs of those individuals serving on the juries. Different results are often reached when criminal and civil trials that involve the same fact situation are held because the jury composition is different and because different legal standards are employed in making judgment. The famous O.J. Simpson criminal murder trial and civil wrongful death trial are examples known to many. In the criminal trial, the prosecution's burden of proof was to show "beyond a reasonable doubt" that the accused had committed the murder. In the civil trial, the standard of proof only required showing liability by a "preponderance of the evidence." Nevertheless, it is a system that has served us well.

Although the outcome of any given case may not be completely predictable, understanding what is actually happening in this process increases substantially one's ability to determine, beforehand, what is considered fair and reasonable. Figure 3.1 depicts a behavioral continuum that can be used in assessing what is fair and reasonable conduct. As the current time frame suggests, actions and beliefs common and acceptable to most people are generally considered reasonable; and

FIGURE 3.1. ASSESSING WHAT IS FAIR AND REASONABLE CONDUCT

Time Frame:	Emerging	Current	Expired
Nature of the conduct or belief	New actions and beliefs unknown or unacceptable to most people	Actions and beliefs common and acceptable to most people	Actions and beliefs that have been rejected or replaced by most people

Predictable Unreasonable	Unpredictable (Gray)	Predictable Reasonable	Unreasonable (Gray)	Predictable Unreasonable

it is very predictable that a jury will treat them that way. It is also very predictable that a jury will find conduct located in either the emerging or expired time frame of the continuum as unreasonable because the conduct constitutes behavior that is unacceptable to most people. Where most difficulties arise is when questions of conduct are located between the current and the extreme outer time frames—falling into areas best described as being gray. Conduct in this range of the continuum may or may not be seen as acceptable. Consequently, it becomes less predictable to judge how a jury of one's peers might react to the conduct.

The message to school principals and other school officials is that to minimize the likelihood of their behavior or conduct being viewed as unfair or unreasonable, make sure policies and practices mirror what the majority of their peers view as acceptable. For example, in establishing a program of supervision for the playground, it would be well for a school principal to contact other principals whose schools have similar playground configurations to determine the nature of their safety and supervisory plans. Although not foolproof, as it is conceivable that all might be operating at a standard well below what a court of law might find adequate, there is some safety in following the collective experience of one's professional colleagues. This is especially true if those contacted are individuals with a good deal of administrative experience and who enjoy solid reputations for exercising reasonable judgment.

It is also important for school officials to understand some of the other factors, besides an imprecise legal system for determining fairness and reasonableness, that affect society's views of "fair and reasonable." First, standards of reasonableness are subject to change over time. They are a reflection of the tenor of the times. The following is a portion of a 1923 female teacher's contract issued by a local board of education in a small school district located in a western state.

1923 Teachers' Contract

1. Not to get married. This contract becomes null and void if the teacher marries.
2. Not to keep the company of men.

3. To be home between the hours of 8:00 p.m. and 6:00 a.m. unless in attendance at a school function.

4. Not to loiter in downtown ice cream parlors.

5. Not to leave town at any time without the permission of the chairman of the Board of Trustees.

6. Not to smoke cigarettes or to drink wine, beer, or whiskey. This contract becomes null and void if the teacher is caught drinking wine, beer, or whiskey.

7. Not to ride in a carriage with any man except her brother or father.

8. Not to dress in bright colors.

9. Not to dye hair.

10. Not to wear dresses more than two inches above the ankle.

11. To wear at least two petticoats.

12. To clean and scrub the school every week.

Obviously, these standards would not be viewed by the teachers and citizens of today as being fair and reasonable. In fact, they are seen as so extreme as to be laughable and non-sensical. Yet, in 1923 they were apparently very mainstream. In the 1950s, many schools expected that female students and teachers would wear dresses or skirts to school; and it was against the rules in many places for them to wear pants except on certain designated field trips. Today, this rule or practice would be viewed as unreasonable and discriminatory. Time does alter what society considers to be fair and reasonable. Principals who fail to keep up with changes in what the greater community considers appropriate may encounter legal challenges and difficulties.

Second, standards of reasonableness can and do differ from one locale to another. What might be acceptable in a large metropolitan school district may not be acceptable in smaller or rural settings. Community standards do differ, and the law allows for such. A current example might well be found in the controversy over the distribution of condoms in schools to high school- and junior high school-age students. In some communities, this has become a very acceptable and normal procedure. In others communities, it is viewed as an extremely undesirable and offensive practice.

Third, standards of reasonableness vary not only from one locale to another but from one circumstance or set of conditions to another. For example, the precautions that must be taken to avoid injury or other problems in a chemistry lab, auto mechanics shop, or gymnasium are very different than those required in an English or history classroom.

Finally, it is very important to remember that practitioners in any professional field, including school administration, are held to a higher standard of conduct than are lay individuals. Under the law, professional license or certification means that an individual is competent by reason of training and preparation. As a result, this individual is expected to understand and operate by the acceptable standards of the profession and not by the standards that any individual off the street might adopt. Failure to do so is viewed as unreasonable. Accordingly, principals need to understand what the acceptable standards of their profession entail and remain current with respect to them. Many of these standards are partially defined by the law such as procedures for disciplining students, evaluating teachers, evacuating buildings, preparing budgets, and conducting audits.

ACCORDING DUE PROCESS OF LAW

The Fifth Amendment to the United States Constitution, among other things, restricts the federal government's capability to deprive citizens of life, liberty, or property without first according them due process of law. By virtue of the Fourteenth Amendment, the same restrictions are placed on state governments. Because public school principals are by definition state officials, this is a restriction on their authority. Although given no authority to take away life, school principals are in a position to and possess sufficient authority (or power to recommend) to deprive students, staff, and patrons of interests they have in property and liberty.

According to the United States Supreme Court:

The Fourteenth Amendment's procedural protection of property is a safeguard of the security of interests that a person has already acquired in specific benefits. These interests—property interests —may take many forms. Property interests are not created by the Constitution. Rather, they are created and their dimensions are defined from an independent source such as state law—rules or understandings that secure certain benefits and that support claims of entitlement to those benefits.

To have a property interest in a benefit, a person clearly must have more than an abstract need or desire for it. He must have more than a unilateral expectation of it. He must, instead, have a legitimate claim of entitlement to those benefits (*Board of Regents v. Roth*, 1972, pp. 576–577).

The most common examples in a school setting of a property interest that a school principal might seek to deprive a person of are the property interest a teacher or a staff member has in his or her employment contract and a student's state-law granted right to an education. Any attempt to interfere with either an employment contract (e.g., suspension from or termination of) or depriving a student of the right to attend school (e.g., suspension or expulsion) will more than likely invoke the protections of due process.

Liberty interests are a little more difficult to fully define than are property interests. The United States Supreme Court has noted:

While this Court has not attempted to define with exactness the liberty guaranteed by the Fourteenth Amendment, the term has received much consideration, and some of the included things have been definitely stated. Without doubt, it denotes not merely freedom from bodily restraint but also the right of the individual to contract, to engage in any of the common occupations of life, to acquire useful knowledge, to marry, to establish a home and bring up children, to worship God according to the dictates of his own conscience, and generally enjoy

those privileges long recognized as essential to the
orderly pursuit of happiness by free men (*Meyer v.
Nebraska*, 1923, p. 399).

While the United States Supreme Court may not wish or
be able to define liberty interests with "exactness," courts, including the Supreme Court, have made it clear that liberty interests do include the freedoms found within the Bill of
Rights as well as many unenumerated fundamental rights
that are "essential to the orderly pursuit of happiness by free
men."

As noted by Valente (1994, p. 223),

It may be said that liberty interests are implicated
whenever government action threatens to suppress or deter their exercise (e.g., by censoring or
punishing freedom of speech or by stigmatizing an
employee's honor, integrity, or reputation in ways
that foreclose his or her opportunities to obtain
professional employment).

Similarly, the potential exists for a student's liberty interests to be implicated anytime a restriction is placed on the
student's exercise of free speech, freedom of association, exercise of religious beliefs, and so forth.

It is important to remember that the Fifth and Fourteenth
Amendment Due Process clauses don't preclude state officials from restricting or even denying an individual his or her
property and liberty interests. These amendments simply require that the individual be afforded due process of law before any deprivation be extracted. For government to pursue
its legitimate role and lawful functions, including the educational process, there will arise in the natural course of events
conflicts between an individual's property and liberty interests and the power of the state to carry out its mandate. For
example, a student has a property interest in attending school
and a liberty interest in the protection of his or her reputation.
Yet, if the student becomes so unruly that it disrupts the effective functioning of the school and/or threatens the health
and safety of others, the state becomes unable or obstructed
from fully carrying out its responsibilities. When these conflicts arise, there has to be a system for balancing the interests

of the two parties. The Founding Fathers fearing that the size and power of government (their fear obviously based on their prior experience with the British monarchy) would give a natural advantage to the government in any conflict with an individual citizen, expressly established a system that they hoped would compensate for this imbalance. In short, the Due Process clause was designed to restrict government from operating in an unreasonable, arbitrary, capricious manner in relation to the fundamental rights of individuals. This is a marvelous concept of our American form of democracy. Yet, it can sometimes be frustrating to school principals and other educational and government officials because of the added time and effort it takes to carry it out. When seen and understood for what it is designed to do, school principals should be fully committed to preserving and safeguarding it.

Over time, the courts have interpreted the due process clauses as having two elements. One is substantive, and the other is procedural. Accordingly, courts often speak of substantive due process and procedural due process. Substantive due process refers to that part of the law which defines or regulates rights (i.e., legislation, rules, regulations, policies, executive orders, etc.). A law must have a purpose that is within the power of government to pursue, and the proposed manner of achieving or carrying out the law must be rationally related to the accomplishment of that purpose. To meet the demands of substantive due process, all legislative or regulatory enactments must have a valid objective and a reasonable means for accomplishing the objective. The validity portion demands the affirmative answers to two questions:

♦ Is it within my scope of authority?

♦ Is it contrary to existing rules and regulations (law) of a higher order?

The reasonableness portion demands to know if the means of accomplishing the objective is fit and appropriate to the end in view. This refers not only to the technique for accomplishing the legitimate objective, for example, the penalty for disruptive behavior, but to how the rule is written and made known to those who will come under its enforcement. Rules must be clear and free from vague and arbitrary language.

They should not leave individuals guessing as to the peril that may confound them. And they need to be communicated to those affected in a fair and legitimate manner. In some areas of the law, substantive due process demands that government employ the least restrictive means available for accomplishing its objective.

In contrast, procedural due process refers to the method of enforcing rights or obtaining redress for their invasion. In other words, it pertains to the decision-making process followed in determining whether or not a law, rule, or regulation has been violated. Procedural due process is often divided into "formal procedural due process" and anything less. The reason for the distinction is because unlike some legal rules, procedural due process is not a technical conception with a fixed content unrelated to time, place, and circumstances. In determining the exact amount of procedural due process required, one has to first look at the governmental function involved and the individual private interest at stake. Both then must be examined within the context of time, place, and circumstance. For example, the teacher who deprives a child of the child's chewing gum while in the classroom is viewed very differently than the board of education about to involuntarily terminate a teacher's contract. In the first instance, the law requires little, if any, procedural due process. In the second case, all or most procedural protections must be accorded.

The most fundamental elements of procedural due process are:

+ the right to a notice of the right one is about to be denied and a statement of the reasons or charges as to why the deprivation is about to occur, and

+ the right to respond to those charges.

Formal procedural due process includes a number of other elements including such things as a fair hearing before an impartial body, sufficient time to prepare a defense, the right to refute the charges, the right to present contrasting evidence, the right to confront accusers, the right to legal counsel, and the right to judicial appeal. The protections afforded an individual accused of murder would, for example, include the full range of procedural due process protections provided under the Constitution's due process clauses.

Compliance with the requirements of procedural due process takes time, money, and effort. Its nonprecise nature means that school principals need to be informed as to the degree of procedural due process required in carrying out various deprivations. This is part of learning and remaining current with the educational law knowledge base. However, an important rule of thumb is that the greater the individual interest or expectation at stake, the greater the procedural due process required. Thinking of this relationship as a balancing scale (Figure 3.2) where individual entitlements and rights are balanced against governmentally provided safeguards, helps keep things in proper perspective. Finally, although some deprivations such as the earlier illustration of gum chewing in the classroom are seen as *de minimis* under the law and require no procedural due process action at all, real commitment to according due process is characterized by a dedication or promise to treat everyone fairly and with dignity. Fairness as a minimum requires giving others an opportunity to be heard.

ASSURING EQUAL PROTECTION OF THE LAW

Equality before the law is another critical dimension of a democratic society. The concept of equality appeared early in our nation's history. The Declaration of Independence, for example, declared that "all men are created equal." Today, that principle is well embodied in our laws. Equal protection guarantees are found in the federal Constitution as well as in most, if not, all state constitutions.

The Fourteenth Amendment to the United States Constitution declares that no state shall "deny to any person within its jurisdiction the equal protection of the laws" (US Const, Amend XIV). This constitutional guarantee provides that no person or class of persons shall be denied the same protection of the laws as is enjoyed by other persons or other classes in like circumstances. Commenting on this form of constitutional protection, LaMorte (1996, p. 9) writes that "the principal idea inherent in equal protection, as in due process, is the concept of fairness." Menacker (1987, p. 208) adds to this

FIGURE 3.2. DETERMINING THE DEGREE OF DUE PROCESS

Entitlement
and Rights

Due Process
Requirements

MINOR

MINIMAL

ORDINARY

The larger the na-
ture and weight of
the entitlement or
right, the greater
the amount of due
process that is re-
quired to keep the
scales in balance

INTERMEDIATE

SUBSTANTIAL

FORMAL

thought by noting that "the general idea of equal protection is that the law does not favor or work against any classification of people for reasons of favoritism, prejudice, or bias. The law is to be impartially administered." However, it should be pointed out that complete equality is impossible to achieve and that some forms of discrimination are actually beneficial to the whole of society. In addition, it is important to understand and remember that the Fourteenth Amendment is not designed to provide protection from all discrimination but only those government-imposed forms of discrimination that lack sufficient justification. The fact of the matter is that schools regularly and lawfully engage in classification practices that discriminate. Examples of factors or traits used in such classification practices include age, residency, behavior, academic readiness, and gender. When such classifications are established and found legally justifiable, it is critical that school officials understand and remember that if a benefit is rendered to one person within the classification, all within that classification must receive the benefit equally; and if one person within the classification is deprived of a benefit, all within that classification must be deprived equally (LaMorte, 1996, p. 9).

Because the charge of equal protection is essentially not to discriminate or treat individuals or classes of individuals differently, a critical question in administering and understanding the concept of equal protection of the laws is: "What justification lawfully permits or allows for the unequal or discriminatory treatment of individuals under the federal Constitution's Fourteenth Amendment?" The United States Supreme Court has provided answers to this question by crafting three different tests depending on the trait or right forming the basis of the discrimination.

The first, or basic, test is referred to as the *rational basis test*. It simply requires that laws or decisions of government officials have some reasonable relationship between the enactment or action and some legitimate governmental purpose. For example, a board of education may enact a policy that requires children to have reached five years of age on or before September 1 before being allowed to begin kindergarten. The policy obviously excludes and discriminates against children whose birthdays come after the designated date. This may not be well received by some school patrons who consider their children to be intellectually and socially ready to start school but who cannot enroll them because their birthdays come after the cut-off date. Thus, the policy may not be popular or wise in the eyes of some. Yet, in order not to violate the demands of equal protection, the board need only provide some rationale or set of reasons justifying its decision. In this case, the board might simply put forward data that indicates that the vast majority of students are not developmentally ready to start kindergarten before the age of five and that administratively and pedagogically the school system can best accommodate students through a yearly rather than daily admission pattern. (It should be noted that the rational basis test has multiple applications in the law and is used in situations other than equal protection challenges. Most commonly, it is used when the legality of statutes is challenged or the decision of an administrative body is questioned.)

The second test is the *strict scrutiny test*. This test is only used by the courts when the classification under consideration is suspect or affects a fundamental interest. Clearly established suspect classifications include those based on race and ethnicity. Fundamental interests are those rights which have their source and which are explicitly or implicitly guaranteed in the federal constitution (Black, 1990, p. 674). Under this test, the government is required to demonstrate that its action was necessary and narrowly tailored to meet a compelling governmental interest. A compelling interest is one which a state is forced or obliged to protect. The strict scrutiny test creates a standard or requirement which is extremely difficult for a state governmental entity to achieve. In fact, if a complaining party can convince a court that his or her case is to be judged on the basis of the strict scrutiny test, that party will usually win the lawsuit.

Because the rational basis test is generally a relatively easy test for the state to comply with and strict scrutiny cases are normally quite rare and more difficult to establish, the Supreme Court crafted a third test known as the *substantial basis test* or *intermediate scrutiny test*. Under this test, the government is required to demonstrate that the challenged classification bears a substantial relationship to an important governmental interest or, in other words, one of much significance and consequence. This test has been particularly employed in cases involving gender and alienage. For example, in 1975, the Texas legislature amended its statutes to withhold from local school districts any state funds used for the education of children who were illegal aliens. Additionally, the revised statute authorized local school districts to deny admission to this particular class of individuals. The essence of the rationale given for this discriminate treatment was that the students were in the country illegally and were consuming limited state resources. The United States Supreme Court ruled that although undocumented aliens are not a suspect classification and education is not a fundamental right under the United States Constitution, more than a *rational basis* argument would need to be presented to justify the unequal treatment of this particular classification of students; a *substantial state interest* would have to be shown. The court ruled that the state's arguments did not reach that level. In so ruling, the court seemed to be moved by the severity of the punishment, which was aimed at children who were innocent of the unlawful conduct of their parents. (See *Plyler v. Doe*, 1982). The case also illustrates that the Equal Protection Clause of the Fourteenth Amendment applies not just to citizens, but to all persons residing within a state (as per the language of the amendment).

Like the concept of due process of law, which attempts to balance rights and entitlements with measures of increased or decreased procedural and substantive safeguards, equal protection is a balancing act. As Figure 3.3 illustrates, the effort is to balance personal deprivations against governmental interests. The larger the deprivation, the greater the governmental justification that is required.

As important as federal and state constitutional equal protection clauses are in assuring and promoting equality under the law, they are not the only source providing protection for this important legal concept. Many federal and state civil rights statutes have been passed over the years; and there are numerous court cases giving support, interpretation, and direction to the administration of these acts.

FIGURE 3.3. DETERMINING THE DEGREE
OF EQUAL PROTECTION

Nature of the
Deprivation

Governmental
Justification
Required

ORDINARY

RATIONAL
ARGUMENT

The larger the
nature and weight
of the deprivation,
the greater the
justification
required

SIGNIFICANT

SUBSTANTIAL
INTEREST

AFFECTS A
FUNDAMENTAL
INTEREST OR SUSPECT
CLASSIFICATION

COMPELLING
INTEREST

Such statutes have been designed to protect against unequal treatment by reason of such factors as age, salary, handicap, gender, and health condition. Although it is beyond the scope of this book to inform school principals of all these particular statutes and cases, they form an important part of the educational law knowledge base with which principals should be familiar.

RESPECTING INDIVIDUAL RIGHTS AND FREEDOMS

Another essential dimension of our democratic heritage in the United States has been the identification of and commitment to the preservation of certain fundamental rights and freedoms for individuals. This has come in the form of limitations and constraints placed on the government. The enumeration of these rights and privileges is found in constitutional and statutory documents at both federal and state levels. Although we consider the Bill of Rights (the first ten amendments to the United States Constitution) as being the most important and fundamental list of enumerated rights, they were neither the first nor are they the only list of important individual freedoms which government must respect. Even before the Declaration of Independence was signed, the Virginia Bill of Rights, for example, had been drafted and adopted by the Virginia Convention of 1776. Many of the provisions found in that document ultimately made their way into the United States Constitution in one form or another. The constitutional and statutory provisions of most states contain important declarations preserving and/or granting individuals certain rights and freedoms.

It is incumbent on school principals and other educational officials to become acquainted with these constitutional and statutory provisions. Those contained in the federal Bill of Rights are, of course, essential for all school principals to know and respect because they are applicable throughout the land. The most pertinent of these constitutional provisions to the management of schools are found within the First, Fourth, Fifth, and Ninth Amendments and include:

- Freedom of religion (amend I)
- Freedom of speech (amend I)
- Freedom of the press (amend I)
- Right to peaceably assemble (amend I)
- Right to petition government for a redress of grievances (amend I)
- Right of citizens to be secure in their persons, houses, papers, and effects from unreasonable searches and seizures (amend IV)
- Right of citizens in criminal cases not to be compelled to be a witness against themselves (amend V)
- Right of due process of law (amend V)
- Right of just compensation for private property taken for public purposes (amend V)
- Right to personal privacy (amend IX)

The original Bill of Rights placed limitations on the federal government. However, by virtue of the Fourteenth Amendment to the United States Constitution, all of the above freedoms and rights must also be observed by state governments. The Fourteenth Amendment also provides the right to equal protection of the laws.

Although not labeled as "fundamental rights and freedoms," there are a number of statutory provisions at the federal and state levels that grant added rights and freedoms to individuals. Many of these statutes significantly impact the operation and management of public schools. Therefore, it is critical that school principals be acquainted with them. Although not listed in any order of importance, 20 of the more important federal statutory provisions that affect all public school principals are:

- The Age Discrimination in Employment Act of 1967 (29 U.S.C. §623).

  An act prohibiting "an employer...to fail or refuse to hire or to discharge any individual or otherwise discriminate against any individual with respect to his compensation, terms, conditions, or privileges of employment, because of such individual's age."

- The Americans with Disabilities Act of 1990 (42 U.S.C. §12101).

An act declaring that "subject to the provisions of this title, no qualified individual with a disability shall, by reason of such disability, be excluded from participation in or be denied the benefits of services, programs, or activities of a public entity, or be subjected to discrimination by such entity.

- The Asbestos School Hazard Detection and Control Act of 1980 (20 U.S.C. §3601).

An act requiring every public and private school in the country to test for the presence of asbestos in their facilities and to mitigate the risks of flaking and crumbling asbestos. This act was followed by *The Asbestos Hazard Emergency Response Act of 1986* (15 U.S.C. §2641), which is actually part of the *Toxic Substance Control Act* and which requires the Environmental Protection Agency to establish regulations and inspection standards and local school districts to develop management plans to guide the mitigation of the asbestos problem in schools. The *Toxic Substance Control Act* also contains provisions to reduce the exposure to lead-based paint (15 U.S.C. §2681) and the abatement of indoor radon gas (15 U.S.C. §2667).

- Civil Rights Act of 1871 (42 U.S.C. §1983).

An act extending personal liability to public officials who violate the constitutional rights of citizens of the United States or other persons within the jurisdiction thereof.

- Civil Rights Act of 1866 (42 U.S.C. §1981) as amended by the Civil Rights Act of 1991 (Pub. L. No. 102-166, 105 Stat. 1071 (1992)).

  An act prohibiting race or ethnicity discrimination in contract construction, terms, conditions, performance, benefits, modification, or termination.

- Civil Rights Act of 1964—Title VI (42 U.S.C. §2000d).

  An act declaring that "No person in the United States, shall, on the ground of race, color, or national origin, be excluded from participation in, be denied the benefits of, or be subjected to discrimination under any program or activity receiving Federal financial assistance."

- Civil Rights Act of 1964—Title VII (42 U.S.C. §2000e-2(a)).

  An act prohibiting discrimination in employment on the basis of race, color, religion, sex, or national origin.

- Civil Rights Restoration Act of 1987 (20 U.S.C. §1687).

  An act declaring that if any part of an educational entity receives federal funds, all of the operations of the entity must comply with Title VI and Title VII of the Civil Rights Act of 1964 and Section 504 of the Rehabilitation Act of 1973.

- Copyright Act (17 U.S.C. §101 *et seq.*).

  An act granting intangible rights to an author or originator of an article or literary work.

- Equal Access Act of 1984 (20 U.S.C. §4071).

  An act making it "unlawful for any public secondary school which receives Federal financial assistance and which has a limited open forum to deny equal access or a fair opportunity to, or discriminate against, any students who wish to conduct a meeting within that limited open forum on the basis of religious, political, philosophical, or other content of the speech at such meetings."

- Equal Educational Opportunities Act of 1974 (20 U.S.C. §1701).

  An act mandating that no state shall deny educational opportunities to an individual on account of his or her race, color, sex, or national origin.

- Equal Pay Act of 1963 (29 U.S.C. §206(d)).

  An act prohibiting unequal payment of wages to men and women for "equal work on jobs, the performance of which requires equal skill, effort, and responsibility and which are performed under similar working conditions."

- Family Educational Rights and Privacy Act of 1974 (also known as FERPA or the Buckley Amendment) (20 U.S.C. §1232g).

  An act establishing specific parental and student rights relative to the content, use, and distribution of student records that are maintained by any institution receiving federal funds.

- Gun-Free Schools Act of 1994 (20 U.S.C. §8921).

  An act requiring states receiving federal funds to have a state law which requires local educational agencies to expel from school for a period of not less than one year a student who brings a firearm to school.

- Homeless Assistance Act (Steward B. McKinney Act) (42 U.S.C. §11431).

  An act ensuring "that each child of a homeless individual and each homeless youth has equal access to the same free, appropriate public education, including a public preschool education, as provided to other children and youth."

- Individuals with Disabilities Education Act (formerly the Education for All Handicapped Children Act of 1975) (20 U.S.C. §1401).

  An act assuring all children with disabilities access to a publicly supervised and funded education appropriate to their individual needs in the least restrictive environment.

- Pregnancy Discrimination Act of 1978 (42 U.S.C. §2000e(k)).

  An act modifying Title VII of the Civil Rights Act of 1964 by extending the prohibition of employment discrimination on the basis of gender to include discrimination on the basis of pregnancy and child birth.

- Protection of Pupil Rights Act of 1974 (20 U.S.C. §1232h).

  An act requiring that parents be allowed to inspect or examine all instructional materials used in connection with any survey, analysis, or evaluation associated with experimental or research programs involving new or unproven teaching methods or techniques. The act was subsequently amended to require parental consent before a minor student can be submitted to psychiatric or psychological testing or treatment, or before being required to participate in any survey, analysis, or evaluation whose primary purpose is to reveal information concerning specified areas relating to personal behavior, beliefs, or family relationships.

- Section 504 of the Rehabilitation Act of 1973 (29 U.S.C. §794).

  An act declaring that "no otherwise qualified individual with a disability...shall, solely by reason of her or his disability, be excluded from participation in, be denied the benefits of, or be subjected to discrimination under any program or activity receiving Federal financial assistance...."

♦ Title IX of the Education Amendments of 1972 (20 U.S.C. §1681).

An act prohibiting any educational program or activity receiving federal funds from treating students unequally on the basis of sex.

The meaning of and managerial implications for school principals of the fundamental rights and freedoms enumerated in the Bill of Rights are found in the opinions of appellate courts as judges attempt to resolve the inevitable conflicts that arise when public educational interests clash with individual interpretations of these rights and freedoms. Statutory provisions generally provide more specific managerial direction than constitutional provisions and have the added benefits of the accompanying rules and regulations formulated by federal administrative agencies. They, too, however, are subject to court interpretation as unresolved disputes arise.

These lengthy lists of federal constitutional and statutory provisions serve as an indicator of the complexity and enormity of the knowledge base found within the legal and regulatory environment in which school principals work. Despite what may seem to be an impossible task, principals need to develop and maintain a respect for and a compliance with the rights and freedoms guaranteed American citizens. By so doing, legal risks and liability will be significantly reduced; preventative law will be practiced and the ideals of a democratic society will be taught and preserved.

SUGGESTED ACTIVITIES

♦ Select a school policy or supervisory plan operating within your own school and test its reasonableness and adequacy by comparing it with similar policies or plans of other schools.

♦ Conduct an audit of your school's policies and procedures to determine their sufficiency in light of procedural and substantive due process requirements.

- Identify the policies and procedures operating within your school that discriminate between or among various students (i.e., those based on such things as age, academic ability, or gender) and then determine the basis on which these distinctions are made. Evaluate those reasons in light of equal protection requirements.

- Search your state statutory and administrative codes for specific rights and freedoms that are provided students and parents of students attending the public schools in your state.

REFERENCES

Black, H.C., J.R. Nolan, J.M. Nolan-Haley, et al. (1990). *Black's Law Dictionary* (6th ed.). St. Paul, MN: West Publishing Co.

Board of Regents v. Roth, 408 U.S. 564 (1972).

LaMorte, M.W. (1996). *School Law: Cases and Concepts* (5th ed.). Needham Heights, MA: Allyn & Bacon.

McCarthy, M.M., B.L. Bull, R.A. Quantz, and G.P. Sorenson. (1994). "Domain VI: Legal and ethical dimensions of schooling," in W.K. Hoy (ed.), *Educational Administration: The UCEA Document Base* (Vol. 2). New York: McGraw-Hill; 1261–1522.

Menacker, J. (1987). *School Law: Theoretical and Case Perspectives.* Englewood Cliffs, NJ: Prentice-Hall.

Meyer v. Nebraska, 262 U.S. 390 (1923).

Plyler v. Doe, 457 U.S. 202 (1982).

Valente, W.D. (1994). *Law in the Schools* (3rd ed.). New York: Macmillan Publishing company

4

LAW AS AN
INSTRUMENT OF
ADMINISTRATIVE
DECISION MAKING

INTRODUCTORY OBSERVATIONS

School principals often believe that familiarity with the educational law knowledge base, including its underlying values and concepts, is critical to guaranteeing compliance with legal requirements. Although this is important, particularly in areas where mandatory performance is required, an understanding of how to make decisions involving legal (or potential) problems is a skill that should be equally cultivated by school principals.

Many of the problems faced on a regular basis by school principals which are completely or partially legal in nature can't be totally addressed with an exact or fixed legal response. School principals, for the most part, are "the law" to those with whom they serve and work. Principals formulate many of the rules, give interpretation to most laws and regulations, and generally administer the law by serving as the prosecutor, judge, and jury. Hundreds of the decisions that a school principal makes involve legal issues, yet, most of these decisions are handled as an act of personal judgment. A judge will not appear on the scene and take over the matter. Some predetermined "quick fix" will not emerge to dictate the outcome. In most instances, however, there are some legal parameters, relevant laws and regulations, and precedent-setting cases that a principal can call on for guidance. Skill in applying these resources to the decision-making process is an essential element in effectively working in a legal and regulatory environment. Without the development of legal decision-making skills, a school principal is really running by the proverbial "seat of the pants," enhancing the risk for serious legal problems and, more importantly, failing to serve the students, staff, and patrons in a fully professional manner. The few who have survived in the past who have not developed these skills can only thank a tolerant community, informed colleagues, sheer good luck, or, more likely, a revered gift of "common sense." The latter is still a wonderful resource to be relied on when knowledge is scant or when time doesn't allow for the luxury of obtaining relevant information. Yet, with the growth and complexity of education law and the propensity for people to litigate their differences, these measures are less and less likely to prove adequate in the future, and certainly don't promote a preventative law approach.

In addition, most of the nonlegal serious problems, complex questions, and sensitive issues faced by school principals, regardless of their nature (i.e., pedagogical, financial, human relations, etc.), have elements attached to them that can be better understood and treated through a legal perspective. School principals are generally trying to advance what is good for society and/or to promote important community values and social objectives. In this sense, school principals share a common purpose with those who make and administer the laws in a democratic society. Therefore, the utilization of "legal lenses" may help better frame alternative responses and result in improved overall decision making.

DECISION MAKING IN SCHOOL ADMINISTRATION

Decision making has been described by Herbert Simon (1960, p. 1) as being "synonymous with managing." Many consider it to be the most important of all administrative activities. As noted by Gorton and Snowden (1993, p. 3), "Intuition and experience often form the basis of administrative decision making. Yet, they are seldom sufficient." Several theories or views of decision making have been developed over the years to explain this activity and, more importantly, to enhance the effectiveness of the process thereby improving the outcome. Perhaps the best known of these theories is the "scientific" or normative prescriptive decision-making approach. Figure 4.1 depicts a version of this model. Gorton and Snowden (1993, pp. 3–4), describe the model as a

> process that begins with a problem or need that the administrator then logically addresses by engaging in a series of sequential steps, culminating in an effective solution or decision....The...approach is concerned with what ought to be done and with prescribing actions designed to produce the best solution....This rational bureaucratic view assumes that administrators function in a closed system, a bureaucracy, characterized by task specification, rigid adherence to written rules and regulations, and formal hierarchal control. Decision making in this structured context is seen through the lens of the decision maker, a supposedly rational administrator. The decision-making process emphasizes solutions to problems and outcome of choice among alternatives with regard to clearly delineated objectives accomplished by following specific tasks and steps.

Critics of this theory argue that the real world in which school administrators operate isn't as rational as the model would have it be. They contend that the real world is much too dynamic and complex and that there are too many unforeseen and unpredictable factors for it to work effectively. They also believe that most administrators don't have or take the time to engage in information-gathering and at best are

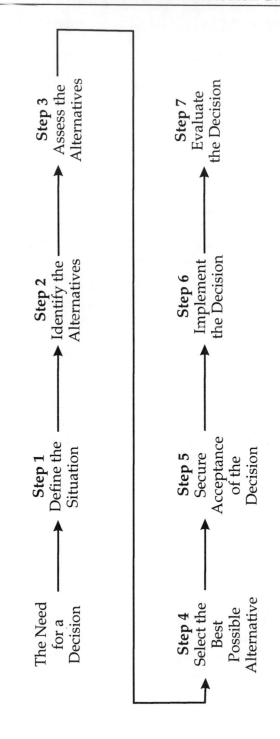

FIGURE 4.1. MAJOR STEPS IN DECISION MAKING

The Need for a Decision

Step 1
Define the Situation

Step 2
Identify the Alternatives

Step 3
Assess the Alternatives

Step 4
Select the Best Possible Alternative

Step 5
Secure Acceptance of the Decision

Step 6
Implement the Decision

Step 7
Evaluate the Decision

Source: Richard A. Gorton and Petra E. Snowden (1993). *School Leadership and Administration* (4th ed.), Madison WI: Brown and Benchmark Publishers; p. 8.

left to "muddle" through with whatever their "common sense," natural reasoning, and/or experience allow. Still others criticize the model for focusing simply on the administrator as the decision maker and not allowing for group involvement.

These and other criticisms have resulted in modified versions of the basic normative model. Three described by Gorton and Snowden (1993) are the participatory decision-making model, the strategic decision-making approach, and differentiated decision making. Although beyond the scope of this book to describe each modified approach, a fair summary is that they each attempt to address the arguments of the critics of the normative approach by modifying the technique or process by which the basic model is utilized and/or made operational. Regardless of the approach, it is important to note that they all place a value on knowledge and its capability of contributing to the improvement of the decision-making process. They also generally preserve a sequential approach to decision making while building in and providing for greater flexibility for identifying who does what and when they do it. The process of legal reasoning and decision making presented in the next section should be seen as an approach designed to be consistent with all these normative models of decision making. Although the model is described as being carried out by a single administrator (school principal), it can be used by a group and easily made a part of a strategic decision-making approach.

LEGAL DECISION-MAKING MODEL

The legal decision-making model is found in Figure 4.2. It is virtually identical to the basic, normative decision-making model except that it contains three additional steps (2, 3, and 4). These steps are serious intellectual exercises that draw on the decision maker's ability to utilize the educational law knowledge base, perform basic legal research activities, and to assess legal problems in light of both the related law and the contemporary context. A description of each step follows.

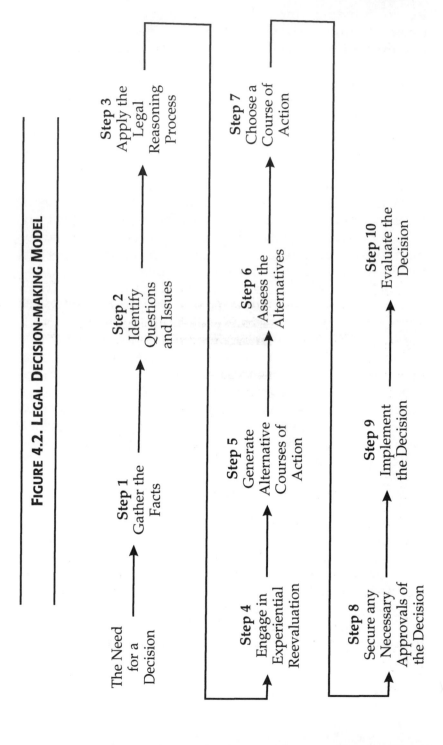

FIGURE 4.2. LEGAL DECISION-MAKING MODEL

The Need for a Decision

Step 1 Gather the Facts

Step 2 Identify Questions and Issues

Step 3 Apply the Legal Reasoning Process

Step 4 Engage in Experiential Reevaluation

Step 5 Generate Alternative Courses of Action

Step 6 Assess the Alternatives

Step 7 Choose a Course of Action

Step 8 Secure any Necessary Approvals of the Decision

Step 9 Implement the Decision

Step 10 Evaluate the Decision

STEP 1: GATHERING THE FACTS

When the need for a decision arises, a critical first step is to define the situation. In a legal context, this is described as gathering the facts. The importance of this step is often overlooked. As Jacobstein, Mersky, and Dunn (1994, p. 16) observe:

> Inexperienced legal researchers tend to skim over the facts and begin researching. No productive research can be done outside a particular fact pattern. Most research, and controversy, is over facts, not law, and cases are most often distinguished on the facts....You will save time, and will achieve more accuracy, if you initially take the time to identify the relevant facts and write them down in some narrative form.

Although offered as counsel to beginning legal researchers, it applies equally to administrative decision makers.

A long-standing technique in legal circles for assembling and analyzing the facts is the "TARP RULE" (Jacobstein, Mersky, & Dunn, 1994, p. 16):

> **T — Thing** or subject matter (including the place or property involved);
>
> **A** — Cause of **action** (claim that might be asserted) or ground of defense;
>
> **R — Relief** sought;
>
> **P — Persons** or **parties** involved.

The application of this rule is illustrated by this hypothetical situation:

> *Situation:* A school principal is confronted by a parent who charges that his daughter is being stalked and tormented at school by a male student who persists in grabbing and kissing her against her wishes. The parent reports that his daughter is frightened and scared of the pursuer and doesn't want to come to school because of him.

In this hypothetical situation, the **thing** or subject matter is the unwelcome annoyance or behavior of the male student on school grounds. The cause of **action**, could be a claim that the school is unlawfully allowing a student to interfere with the safety and well-being of another. The **relief** being sought isn't described, but it might be a simple request that the school protect the daughter from the male student, that the male student be punished by the school and restrained from repeating the act, or that monetary compensation from the school district be made for a violation of civil rights. The **person** or **parties** involved include the girl, the boy, and possibly others not mentioned in the scenario.

The situational description is, obviously, factually insufficient to justify any immediate decision making or action on the part of the school principal. The seriousness of the father's complaint, however, demands that additional facts and evidence be gathered. Utilizing the framework found in the TARP rule, the principal could easily begin assembling more facts by asking the father some important questions. Then, depending on the father's answers and intentions, the gathering of additional facts and information could be planned and carried out. Some examples of questions that might be asked of the father are:

♦ *Thing*

In what locations of the school, has this harassment occurred (where)?

Has this been a persistent or one-time event (how often)?

What seems to have provoked the behavior (why)?

Have others been involved (who)?

What exactly has the boy done (what)? Has the girl been injured or suffered harm beyond her fear of the boy? If so, what is the nature and extent of the injury (what)?

+ *Action*

At this point in time, no questions may be necessary with respect to this factor unless the parent
expresses intent to refer the matter to an attorney
or to sue the school district. If brought up by the
parent, an attempt should be made to ascertain
the nature of the legal claim or action the parent
intends to pursue.

+ *Relief*

What is it that you would like the school to do
(what)?

+ *Persons or Parties*

Who has actually been involved (i.e., students,
teachers, staff members, outsiders, etc.) (who)? In
what ways (what)? Are there witnesses to the
boy's behavior? If so, who are they (who)?

If a teacher has been told, what was the teacher's
reaction (what)? What did the teacher do to try to
resolve the matter (what)?

Have any others been bothered by this boy
(who)? Is this the only boy who is behaving this
way (who)?

As should be obvious from the questions suggested, one
constructive technique for gathering facts is to utilize the
what, when, who, where, how, and *why* questions. Learning to
effectively gather information and evidence is a critical skill
that principals need to develop to support many aspects of
their work, not just that which is related to the legal and regulatory environment. However, the accumulation of evidence
in support of factual situations (that which really took place
or which is taking place) is absolutely critical when dealing
with issues and events that have serious legal overtones. A
simple study of case law reveals that where evidence is weak,
cases tend to be lost; where evidence is strong, cases are generally won. The following list of characteristics of good and
poor evidence is based on an examination of actual court
cases involving public schools. Principals should learn to dis-

cern the difference and seek to collect evidence that will be meaningful and useful.

- ◆ Good evidence demands
  - Things of material substance
    - Oral testimony
    - Letters
    - Documented Complaints
    - Official records
    - Written evaluations
    - Certificates
    - Recorded observations
    - Witnesses
    - Written reprimands
    - Recorded incidents
    - Memoranda
    - Court and other public records
    - Policies and procedures
    - Statutes
    - Minutes of conferences and meetings
    - Personnel and student files
  - Details
    - Names
    - Dates
    - Times
    - Location(s)
    - Description of conduct
    - Parties involved
    - Nature of incident
    - Circumstances
  - Demonstrated efforts to remediate
  - Established patterns of behavior

- ◆ Good evidence is not
  - • Idle speculation
  - • Fear of something happening
  - • Hearsay or rumors
  - • Personal whims
  - • Conjecture or supposition
  - • Inferences
  - • Guesswork
  - • Personal dislikes
  - • Wishful thinking

STEP 2: IDENTIFYING LEGAL ISSUES AND QUESTIONS

Step 2 is an intellectual exercise that first requires an examination of the gathered facts for the purpose of identifying and extracting from them the critical issues that need to be addressed. The critical issues are then reviewed for the purpose of teasing out the relevant questions that need answering before a course of action can be formulated. As illustrated in Figure 4.3, it is a process not unlike a funnel with two screens where the facts are refined and narrowed into relevant issues and questions and insignificant facts and issues are discarded. Effectively carrying out this process is one of the skills that separates excellent attorneys from average ones. It is also a skill that separates effective decision-making school principals from their less competent peers.

The ability to successfully work through this step is greatly enhanced when at least three things are in place. First, all of the relevant facts have been gathered. As noted in step 1, taking the time to gather the facts is often neglected and can easily come back to haunt the decision-maker. Second, the decision-maker has an up-to-date familiarity with the educational law knowledge base. Even a general awareness of new and developing legislation and court cases will cause one to be more sensitive, reflective, and cautious when processing facts in search of relevant legal issues and questions. Finally, the decision-maker knows where and how to find the law.

FIGURE 4.3. IDENTIFYING LEGAL ISSUES AND QUESTIONS

PROBLEM

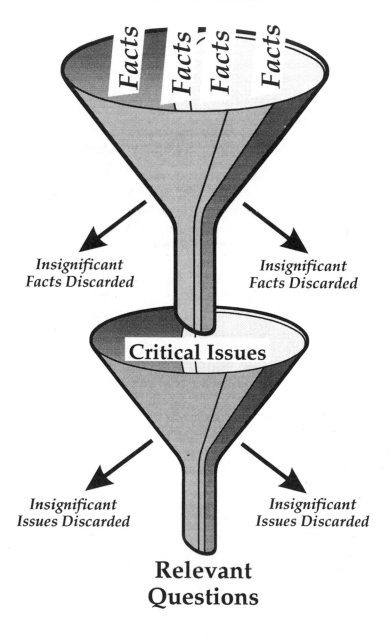

Insignificant Facts Discarded

Insignificant Facts Discarded

Critical Issues

Insignificant Issues Discarded

Insignificant Issues Discarded

Relevant Questions

If the facts have been thoroughly assembled and the decision-maker is familiar with the knowledge base, the critical issues and relevant questions often emerge and are readily identifiable. However, for the new and inexperienced administrator or for one dealing with an unfamiliar legal topic, the task may not be an easy one. The following suggestions are offered for those navigating these waters. First, while applying the funnel concept of Figure 4.3, view the initial process of identifying legal issues (or potential legal issues) as a task of classifying or categorizing the problem into general, and increasingly specific, subject matter areas (Jacobstein, Mersky, & Dunn, 1994, p. 17). Although there is no definitive classification or categorization of educational law topics, textbook writers normally divide educational law into nine areas:

- Church and state
- Discrimination (sometimes referred to or expanded into separate topics of race and/or desegregation)
- Educational program (sometimes referred to as curriculum or instruction and may or may not include church–state)
- Exceptional students (sometimes referred to as students with special needs and special education law)
- Health and safety
- Liability or tort liability
- Organization and governance (sometimes expanded into separate topics of school boards, finance, property, and legal framework of education)
- Personnel management (sometimes referred to or expanded into separate topics of contracts, professional negotiations, teacher rights, and teacher employment)
- Student management (sometimes referred to or expanded into separate topics of student

discipline, classification of students, and student
rights)

Although problems are not always easily categorized, as-
signing a problem to one or more of the branches of educational law often helps narrow the search for critical legal issues. For example, in the hypothetical situation presented in
step 1, the principal might well determine that the problem
fits in the category of health and safety because the girl's well
being and safety seem in jeopardy. Having narrowed the
search for legal issues by placing the problem into what
seems to be a relevant category, the second task of further re-
fining the search (again, think of the narrowing funnel in Figure 4.3) is to review an up-to-date educational law treatise,
looseleaf service, or legal encyclopedia under the topic of
health and safety. If the researcher utilizes the looseleaf publication *Education Law and the Public Schools: A Compendium*
(2nd ed.) (Sperry, Daniel, Huefner, & Gee, 1998), for example,
these topics are listed under the category of Health and
Safety: Child Abuse/Child Sexual Abuse; Contagious Dis-
eases; Drug, Alcohol, and Tobacco Use; Emergencies;
Medically Fragile Students; School Health Issues; and Student Violence. By aligning the nature of the problem with the
titles of the topics, the researcher then looks for those topics
that appear to be relevant to the problem and discards those
that appear not to be relevant. For example, there is nothing
in the known facts to suggest that drugs, alcohol, or tobacco
are part of the problem. Therefore, there is no need to inspect
or read material on that particular topic. However, topics relating more directly to the problem should be perused beginning with the topic that intuitively seems most relevant.

Because the complaint relates to the unwanted kissing
and tormenting of a female student by a male student, the
topic of Child Abuse/Child Sexual Abuse might be examined first. The logic for this choice is that abuse is a synonym
for torment and unwanted kissing could be a form of sexual
abuse. A cursory examination of this topic reveals a section
dealing with "School District Liability for Abuse by Private
Actors" (Sperry, Daniel, Huefner, & Gee, 1998, pp. 116–118).
Reading the section makes it apparent that sexual abuse in
schools by third parties, including other students, is a grow-

ing problem and one that is beginning to receive judicial attention. Thus, one of the possible legal issues that might well fit into the hypothetical situation is sexual abuse in the schools by third parties. This would be even more convincing if in the fact gathering process it had been revealed that the father's intent was to bring legal action against the school under the charge that the school had failed to protect his daughter from suffering sexual harassment at the hands of another student. Assuming for illustrative purposes that such were the case, a third task would be to ask questions that would help school officials better understand their responsibility and obligations in this matter. Thoughtful reflection on the facts and the limited information that was obtained from the *Compendium* will ordinarily produce relevant legal questions. For example, one might naturally ask, "Is unwanted kissing a form of sexual abuse?" Additionally, given that peer-to-peer sexual harassment in schools is a growing problem and having encountered a father who wants school officials to be held liable for such behavior raises the question, "What legal responsibility does a school have regarding peer-to-peer sexual harassment in a school setting?" Once the legal issues and relevant questions are identified and refined, the legal reasoning process takes over.

STEP 3: APPLYING THE LEGAL REASONING PROCESS

Levi (1974, pp. 1–2) described the legal reasoning process as follows:

> The basic pattern of legal reasoning is reasoning by example. It is reasoning from case to case. It is a three-step process described by the doctrine of precedent in which a proposition descriptive of the first case is made into a rule of law and then applied to a next similar situation. The steps are these: similarity is seen between cases; next the rule of law inherent in the first case is announced; then the rule of law is made applicable to the second case.

What Levi describes is a syllogism (or simple deductive reasoning). As a deductive scheme, it consists of a major premise, a minor premise, and a conclusion. *Webster's* dictionary (1986, "syllogism," p. 2315) uses this example to illustrate the concept: "Every virtue is laudable; kindness is a virtue; therefore kindness is laudable."

The legal reasoning process, like identifying legal issues and questions found in step 2, is an intellectual exercise. It demands not only a general familiarity with the educational law knowledge base, but also, in some instances, the skill and ability to find the more precise dimensions of the law through traditional legal research methods and techniques.

In applying the legal reasoning process to the legal questions formulated in step 2, one looks for a case, statute, or regulation (or sometimes a combination of these primary legal sources) that addresses or relates to the questions. In so doing, it is important to bear in mind the hierarchical nature of law, which was explained in Chapter 2. Thus, efforts should focus first on federal statutes and federal court decisions, especially United States Supreme Court decisions. Either through original research or by consulting a good up-to-date educational law reference service, one will quickly find the existence of federal statutes and court cases directly applicable to the two questions posed. Such a search reveals that Title VII of the 1964 Civil Rights Act (42 U.S.C. §2000e-2(a)) provides a definition of sexual harassment and that the United States Supreme Court gives interpretation to its meaning (see *Meritor Savings Bank v. Vinson*, 1986). The definition, among other things, outlaws unwelcome sexual advances that interfere with an individual's work performance or which creates an intimidating, hostile, or offensive work environment. The search also reveals that although Title VII deals with employment practices, Title IX of the Education Amendments of 1972 (20 U.S.C. §1681) prohibits discrimination on the basis of gender in public education programs. Research also reveals that court cases have interpreted this to include the hostile-environment sexual-harassment theory found in Title VII. Thus, applying the legal reasoning formula to the first question, one might conclude that sexual harassment includes unwelcome sexual advances that create an intimidating, hostile, or offensive environment in the school (major premise). The girl did not welcome the boy's sexual advances in trying to kiss her at school (minor premise). Therefore, the boy's conduct constituted sexual harassment (conclusion).

As to the second question regarding what legal responsibility school officials have relative to peer-to-peer sexual harassment in a school setting, a search of federal statutes and court cases indicates that currently there are no United States Supreme Court decisions that deal directly with this question. However, the search does reveal a split among several federal circuit courts over the question of whether school districts and their employees can be held liable under Title IX for student-to-student sexual harassment in a school setting. Thus, technically, the answer to the second legal question developed in step 2 depends on where the school district in the hypothetical situation was located. In some jurisdictions, school officials could possibly be held liable by virtue of a federal court decision, and in others they would not be. Despite this current split in judicial rulings, most administrators committed to taking a preventative legal approach would want to know where the law seems to be heading. A closer examination of the federal Courts of Appeals cases joined with documents from the federal Office of Civil Rights (OCR) seems to suggest that the trend in the law is to hold school districts liable if they knew of the conduct or should have known and took no action to investigate or control it or otherwise showed a reckless indifference to the continuing harassment. Thus, assuming in the hypothetical situation that the father's complaint was the first any school official knew of the problem, the legal reasoning process might read something similar to this: Federal law holds or seems to be moving in a direction of holding school officials liable in cases of peer-to-peer sexual harassment where school officials have been made aware of the problem (reported or observed) and have failed to take appropriate or reasonable action to prevent reoccurrences (major premise). School officials were not aware of any stalking, tormenting, kissing, or any other form of unwelcome sexual harassment before being informed by the father (minor premise). Therefore, in this instance, school officials do not appear to be liable for what has occurred to date, but do need to take steps to prevent future recurrences (conclusion).

The illustration uses federal law as an example, but the same process is followed in applying school rules, district regulations, and state statutes. These sources of law should be examined as thoroughly as federal sources because they often include more detailed requirements and provide greater protection.

NOTE

As this book was going to press, the United States Supreme Court rendered an important decision on a case closely related to the hypothetical problem of peer-to-peer sexual harassment used in this chapter to illustrate the legal decision-making model. The case is *Gebseret et al. v. Lago Vista Independent School District* (1998). It involved the issue of liability of school districts under Title IX in instances where a teacher is guilty of sexually harassing a student. In the written opinion, the court declared, "Until Congress speaks directly on the subject. . .we will not hold a school district liable in damages under Title IX for a teacher's sexual harassment of a student absent actual notice and deliberate indifference" [*Gebseret et al. v. Lago Vista Independent School District*, No. 96-1866, 1998 U.S. LEXIS 4173, at 10].

Because step 3 is essentially concerned with process, *Gebseret's* holding does not in any manner alter the approach and techniques followed in this part of the legal decision-making process. If anything, it lends strong support to the conclusion reached regarding the question of what legal responsibility and liability school officials have relative to in-school peer-to-peer sexual harassment incidents. It also further illustrates the points made earlier in this book that the school law knowledge base is changing on a daily basis, that school officials need to remain constantly aware of new developments in the law, and that understanding the legal process is as, or perhaps more, important as knowing the knowledge base at one given moment in time.

STEP 4: ENGAGING IN EXPERIENTIAL REEVALUATION

The legal reasoning process explained in step 3 is important to the preservation of the *stare decisis* doctrine (to stand by decided cases) and the rule of precedent (once a point of law has been determined by the courts, it is fixed law and can be changed only by competent authority) as described in Chapter 2. Both are very important concepts of law in American society. The logic is that they help to maintain predictability and consistency in the law. However, there is a competing principle that Justice Oliver Wendell Holmes, Jr. (1881/1963) referred to as one giving "life" (p. 5) to the law. This competing principle refers to "experience." McCarthy, Bull, Quantz, and Sorenson (1994, p. 1279) summarize the essence of this principle thus: "...law derives from the customary practices of lived experience and is intended to enhance individual and community life, [but] its application in the common cause must be flexible, historically embedded, and a part of an ongoing process of application, assessment, refinement, and reapplication." As noted in Chapter 2, although courts are bound by the doctrine of *stare decisis* and the rule of precedent, they only decide the fact situation before them. Consequently, a change in time, place, individual(s) involved, technology, knowledge, public values, scientific advancements, sponsorship, organizational structure, and so forth, often leads to such a significant alteration of the facts that the differences in the cases or circumstances sufficiently outweigh the similarities and thus argue for a reconsideration of what the rule of law should be.

Step 4, engaging in experiential reevaluation, is a process of stepping back from the results generated in steps 2 and 3, mulling over the problem in its contemporary context, and allowing the flexibility of onsite personal experience to play into the equation. Out of this process may well come other important questions and conclusions. For example, suppose that the boy in the hypothetical situation was a five- or six-year-old kindergartner. Does this make a difference? An actual case very similar to this drew a great deal of national attention during the 1996–1997 school year when a school principal, abiding strictly by his school district's sexual harassment policies which were crafted in the language of the federal statutes, suspended a young elementary-age boy from school for chasing and kissing young girls on the school's playground. The parents were shocked. People all over the country criticized the principal's action as insensitive, ridiculous, and foolhardy. Some called for his dismissal or resignation. Many argued that a five-year-old boy doesn't even know how to pronounce the words "sexual harassment" much less know what they mean. Some pled for substituting a kind and gentle instructional approach that would help the boy understand that what he did was inappropriate rather than suspending him for reasons he could not understand. Others felt it improper that the boy should go through life having his school records forever state that he was once guilty of sexual harassment. Some even wondered just what would cause a principal to behave in such a bizarre way. Many asked, "Have school principals become slaves to the law?" Society seemed to be pleading for more than just the letter of the law; it seemed to be pleading for the spirit as well.

Step 4 is that part of the legal decision-making model that allows the school principal to identify potential alternative courses of action that stem from what the actual circumstances would dictate is the most reasonable course of action. This step acknowledges that codified law cannot be expected to be applied neatly to every circumstance. Judge Jerome Frank (1930/1970, p. 6) recognized this when he wrote, "Even in a relatively static society, men have never been able to construct a comprehensive, eternized set of rules anticipating all possible legal disputes and settling them in advance."

Step 4, however, should not be seen as an entitlement to disregard the rule of law or established precedent. Nor is it an open license for school principals to do whatever they want; it is often the case that a regulation, statute, or court opinion bears directly on the problem and provides a clear-cut course of action from which a principal may not deviate. Thus, a principal needs to first respect the rule of law and then seek answers in the established body of law.

When the use of step 4 seems appropriate, it should not be exercised in a random or biased manner. Experiential evaluation needs to be grounded and guided by concepts that will lead to the "right thing." In short, moral judgments have to be made. Like the concept of reasonableness which was described in Chapter 2, doing the "right thing" is an abstraction about which there is no total agreement. However, there are approaches that provide a systematic and logical method for analyzing and evaluating current circumstances and conditions. For example, Charles Slater in the May 1996 issue of *Legal Memorandum* (published by the National Association of Secondary School Principals) suggested nine questions that might be asked in developing a sense of what the "right" or "just" response should be. The questions posed in the memorandum together with a short introduction and conclusion were:

SCHOOL LAW: FRIEND OR FOE?

Slave to the Law

...[T]he rule of law does not mean slavery to rigid interpretations. Administrators often pay attention to law (with a small "l") rather than reflect on the ideas of justice and fairness behind Law (with a capital "L"). They apply the law, rule, or policy to the situation but fail to ask the most important question—What is the right thing to do? Merely verbalizing the question can move a decision from a question of expediency to one of fairness. More than knowing the laws, the principal needs to understand the *concept* of law. What is the right thing? There is no clear answer. People disagree. The ambiguity can be frightening.

The Concept of Law: Nine Questions

When difficult decisions have a moral dimension, the concept of Law can provide questions that point the way. Following are nine areas of importance that may be considered in tough moral decisions. Each area has a question that needs an answer.

1. **Respect.** Does the action respect the individual's integrity? Sergiovanni (1992) outlines moral principles that can guide a leader's decisions. These principles go beyond what is legal and

suggest the right thing to do. The first is to treat people as ends in themselves, never as means. . . .The second principle is seeing other positions. We are asked to "Do unto others as you would have them do unto you."

2. **Safety.** What is the best course to ensure everyone's safety?

3. **Student Welfare.** What is good for the student? It may seem odd to put student welfare third when the primary charge of the school is to educate children. This refers to the individual. All students benefit if respect and safety are first.

4. **Fair Warning.** Did the teacher, student, or parent know of the rule that was violated? Rules in student handbooks, published in classrooms, or given to each student are essential to everyone knowing what to expect.

5. **Due Process.** Did the teacher, student, or parent have an opportunity to hear the charge, tell the other side of the story, and appeal to a higher level?

6. **Consistency.** Is the action consistent with what was done for others?

7. **Public Relations Test.** What is the effect of a decision on those not directly involved? A principal should consider the reputation of the school, the reactions of teacher and students, and public perceptions. The television test is useful: If the media hands the principal a microphone and puts a camera before him, how would his decision sound?

8. **Consultation.** What do colleagues say is the right thing to do? Consultation gives new ideas and opportunities to reflect and think out loud. The principal should not have to feel alone in knowing what decisions to make.

9. **Law and Policy.** What laws, rules, and policies apply? This question is last because the law does not tell the right thing to do. Of course, the principal cannot ignore the law and must act consistently with it.

Law for the Principal

The nine questions begin by asking what is right, end by asking what is legal, and are based on the concept of Law that provides fundamental fairness and justice. . . .Knowledge of law without a general understanding of fairness can result in mindless slavery to the law without justice to the individual.

Law can be a friend to the administrator. The best friend is not one who gives gifts or favors but who gives love and support. Laws are not nearly as important as the sense of fair play that stands behind them. (pp. 2–3)[1]

These nine factors and accompanying questions, obviously don't form the only system for making moral judgments regarding educational problems. They represent the beliefs of the author who places high importance on the well-being of the individual student. The daily decisions made by a school administrator reveal the administrator's internal or personal value system (also referred to as a principal's personal administrative/educational philosophy). Given the important role such a system plays in legal and educational decision-making, it deserves thoughtful development and continuing refinement.

In summary, experiential reevaluation is to apply a principal's sense of right and wrong to legal problems for which there is no established law or where the applicable rule of law doesn't seem to best fit the circumstances. A principal's personal value system or educational/administrative philoso-

1. Reprinted by permission from C. Slater (May 1996), "School Law: Friend or Foe?" *A Legal Memorandum,* National Association of Secondary School Principals. For more information concerning NASSP services and/or programs, please call (703) 860-0200.

phy becomes the source for raising these additional questions and for generating alternative courses of action.

Step 5: Generating Alternative Courses of Action

The legal reasoning process (step 3) and experiential reevaluation (step 4) are the means by which alternative courses of action are generated to address the legal issues identified in step 2. If steps 2 and 3 are properly followed, alternative courses of action will naturally emerge. These intellectual exercises derive their results by having asked: "What statutes, regulations, and/or cases are similar to the problem at hand? What do these primary sources of law require or permit be done? If the law is unsettled, in what direction does the law seem to be moving? If there is no primary law addressing the problem, or if the circumstances of the problem are sufficiently unique from the most controlling case or regulation, what is the right thing to do?"

In the hypothetical situation presented in step 1, the legal reasoning process might well have generated a course of action that would have the principal suspend the young boy for an act of sexual harassment. The process of experiential reevaluation might have suggested that circumstances, particularly the tender age of the boy and his inability to fully appreciate the act of sexual harassment, justified another course of action such as working with the parents to help the boy through counseling to understand the inappropriateness of his behavior.

One potential trap for decision-makers at this stage of the decision making process is to believe or think that there are only two alternatives to every decision and that only one must be chosen. Because the processes followed in steps 3 and 4 each tend to generate a single alternative, it is natural for this to occur. This mode of thinking, however, blocks the development of other legitimate alternatives that may emerge and thereby stifles the synergism, creativity, and compromises that could potentially result from combining the best of several alternatives.

In the hypothetical situation, for example, a series of multiple actions might take place which would utilize both alternative courses of action generated in steps 3 and 4 as well as other ideas. Specifically, given that this was a new or first time problem for the school, this particular boy might be treated with counseling and parental help (alternative generated from step 4). Next, a schoolwide program could be launched to teach all children, parents, and staff about the inappropriateness of sexual harassment (an additional alternative). This could then be followed by establishing a zero-tolerance policy for all future cases. This latter action would be in general harmony with the suspension alternative generated in step 3. This compromise plan has a sense of adherence to both the letter and the spirit of the law.

STEPS 6 AND 7: ASSESSING THE ALTERNATIVES AND CHOOSING A COURSE OF ACTION

The heart and purpose of these two steps are to weigh the consequences or at least try to project what the consequences will be for each alternative choice of action and to then make a final decision. Factors that often need to be considered and pertinent questions to be asked regarding each factor include:

- ♦ Legal—Are the legal consequences completely clear?
- ♦ Justice—Is this a fair and reasonable resolution for all concerned?
- ♦ Economic—What are the financial ramifications?
- ♦ Administrative—What are the administrative consequences and requirements?
- ♦ Public Relations—What impact will this have on the good will and support of the community?
- ♦ Prophylactic—Will this help prevent or ward off future problems of this type?
- ♦ Political—Will this receive the support of the board of education?
- ♦ Social—How will it relate to the beliefs, mores, and social practices of the community?

If the alternative choices have been examined and weighed carefully, a "best" option will generally be apparent. However, it should be noted that six of the suggested eight factors used in assessing the alternatives and choosing a course of action relate to things other than law and justice. This speaks to the pragmatic nature and political world in which public school systems operate. Perfect or easy choices are not always available, and sometimes a preferred choice simply cannot be pursued for a variety of reasons. For example, a principal may feel that he or she has the evidence to support a dismissal action against a teacher, but the teacher is intent on challenging the matter in court. Time away from the job together with high legal costs and adverse publicity may well argue for an undeserved and possibly outrageous out-of-court settlement. Is this an abandonment of a good legal solution or the principle of justice?

Yet there may be situations where, because of need or an uncompromising commitment to a moral principle, a principal feels compelled to pursue his or her preferred choice despite the cost or controversy that might arise. For example, a principal might be having a terrible problem with the use of illegal drugs by student athletes and believes that the best way of eliminating or controlling the problem is through random suspicionless drug testing. It is known by legal research (step 3) that testing urine for evidence of illegal drugs is clearly a search under the Fourth Amendment to the United States Constitution and that the prevailing legal test regarding in-school searches is reasonableness. The principal knows or has been advised that random suspicionless tests may or may not be viewed by the courts as reasonable and that such tests won't be popular by a significant proportion of the school community. Also, if the choice is selected and then challenged in the courts, there may be a substantial cost involved in defending the action. However, the principal may feel that the need is great enough to take the risk. Is it courage of convictions or foolishness that prompts such an action? (This was essentially the situation faced by a group of Oregon school officials, and the result was a long legal battle that resulted in the United States Supreme Court upholding their choice of action. The case was *Vernonia School District 47J v. Acton* (1995). Obviously, not all alternative courses of action selected and defended by school officials will result in a

United States Supreme Court decision that upholds their choice of action. Even when a case is successfully defended judicially, there is often a high price to be paid in reduced morale, legal costs, and sheer time and energy.)

Was there an abandonment of a good legal solution or forsaking of the principle of justice in accepting an out-of-court settlement in the first example? Likewise, was the course of action chosen in the second example a true act of courage or foolishness? These questions illustrate that there is no magical solution or formula for choosing the ultimate or perfect course of action. The legal decision-making model does not assure a flawless outcome. What the process does, however, is to bring the best information and thinking to bear on the problem. In the end, the decision-maker must choose and be prepared to accept the consequences of his or her choice. The examples also illustrate another important point. By viewing the law as a tool of administration rather than strictly as a constraint, school officials can, by their choices, become an active player in shaping the legal and regulatory environment in which they operate.

STEP 8: SECURING NECESSARY APPROVALS FOR THE DECISION

Some legal decisions a principal cannot make unilaterally and require the consent of higher authorities. For example, it is usually the case that only a board of education can hire and fire employees. Likewise, principals can generally suspend a student, but expulsion requires board approval. In addition, some situations are so politically charged, or have such broad policy implications, that failing to consult higher authorities is unreasonable and professionally irresponsible. Legal issues of any significance should be reviewed as a matter of routine practice with district officials and the district's legal counsel. School principals can and should be familiar with the educational law knowledge base, but they should not attempt to serve as their own attorneys.

STEP 9: IMPLEMENTING THE DECISION

Once a decision has been made and necessary approvals secured, the success or failure of all preceding steps hinges on the effectiveness with which the decision is carried out. The general decision-making literature speaks of a number of activities generally associated with this step, including planning, organizing, staffing, directing, coordinating, reporting, budgeting, and evaluating (Gorton & Snowden, 1993, p. 13). All these activities are important and the implementor should take them seriously. In a legal context, however, there is another important item to be kept in mind and properly facilitated. This relates to the procedural side of the law, which is as important as the substantive side. Cases are often lost, decisions reversed, or actions negated not because the written or case law failed to support the administrator's intent, but because established and/or required procedures were not followed. As noted in Chapter 3, due process of law was designed to restrict government from operating in an unreasonable, an arbitrary, or a capricious manner. It demands that the manner of achieving or carrying out the law must be rationally related to the accomplishment of that purpose. In nonlegal situations, if the implementation process breaks down, adjustments can often be made without serious penalization. This is not always the case in legal matters. For example, failure to properly inform a faculty member of an intended action such as nonrenewal of a teaching contract can negate the entire process and cause the decision to become null and void.

STEP 10: EVALUATING THE DECISION

This is a step that calls for taking inventory of how well the original problem was resolved, as well as how effectively the legal decision-making process was followed. These are actions to be taken immediately following implementation. Ten questions that might be asked in carrying out this step are:

- ♦ Were the facts adequately and completely gathered?
- ♦ Were the legal issues identified and pertinent legal questions generated?
- ♦ Were the most "on point" or related statutes, regulations, court cases, and school rules identified?

♦ Was a sense of justice or fair play applied to the problem in both generating questions and possible alternative solutions?

♦ Were multiple alternative courses of action generated?

♦ Were the alternative courses of action screened in light of the law, justice, and related pragmatic factors?

♦ Were key individuals consulted, and were necessary approvals obtained?

♦ Was the final decision properly implemented?

♦ How was the decision received?

♦ What has been the effect of the decision and subsequent implementation on the school or educational program?

SUGGESTED ACTIVITIES

♦ Write out the guiding principles (administrative philosophy) that you use as a school administrator in evaluating issues/problems and in making decisions that affect your students and staff. Compare them with those presented by Charles Slater in the May 1996 *Legal Memorandum*.

♦ Take a legal (or potentially legal) problem or issue you are currently facing in your school and work it through the ten steps of the legal decision-making model.

REFERENCES

Frank, J. (1970). *Law and the Modern Mind.* Glouchester, MA: Peter Smith (original work published 1930).

Gebseret et al. v. Lago Vista Independent School District, No. 96-1866, 1998 U.S. LEXIS 4173 (U.S. June 22, 1998).

Gorton, R.A., and P.E. Snowden. (1993). *School Leadership and Administration* (4th ed.). Madison, WI: Brown & Benchmark Publishers.

Gove, P.B., et al. (1986). *Webster's Third New International Dictionary of the English Language Unabridged.* Springfield, MA: Merriam-Webster, Inc.

Holmes, O.W. (1963) (edited by M.D. Howe). *The Common Law.* Boston: Little, Brown, & Company (original work published 1881).

Jacobstein, J.M., R.M. Mersky, and D.J. Dunn. (1994). *Legal Research Illustrated* (6th ed). Westbury, NY: Foundation Press.

Levi, E.H. (1974). *An Introduction to Legal Reasoning.* Chicago: University of Chicago Press.

McCarthy, M.M., B.L. Bull, R.A. Quantz, and G.P. Sorenson. (1994). "Domain VI: Legal and ethical dimensions of schooling," in W.K. Hoy (ed.), *Educational Administration: The UCEA Document Base* (Vol. 2). New York: McGraw-Hill; 1261–1522.

Meritor Savings Bank v. Vinson, 477 U.S. 57 (1986).

Simon, H.A. (1960). *The New Science of Management Decision.* New York: Harper & Row.

Slater, C. (1996, May). "School law: Friend or foe?" in *A Legal Memorandum.* Reston, VA: National Association of Secondary School Principals.

Sperry, D.J., P.T.K. Daniel, D.S. Huefner, and E.G. Gee. (1998). *Education Law and the Public Schools: A Compendium* (2nd ed.). Norwood, MA: Christopher-Gordon Publishers.

Vernonia School District 47J v. Acton, 115 S.Ct. 2386 (1995).

5

LEGAL
DECISION-MAKING
FLOW CHARTS

As noted in Chapter 1, some dimensions of educational law are common to all educators. This includes federal statutes such as those briefly summarized in Chapter 2. It also includes those decisions of the United States Supreme Court that impact the governance and operation of public schools. An awareness of nearly all these cases and a working familiarity with the holdings, tests, and administrative requirements of many of these decisions are essential and critical elements in the preparation of school administrators to administer their schools. Ultimately, laws are what the courts say they are; and decisions of the United States Supreme Court are the laws of the land. The names of these cases become "household" words to those who must abide by their directives. How can a school principal or other school administrator achieve and maintain a working familiarity with this important part of the educational law knowledge base? This chapter provides some recommendations and ideas that are designed to answer this question.

MAINTAINING FAMILIARITY WITH
COURT DECISIONS

The suggestions made in Chapter 2 relative to becoming familiar with and maintaining a knowledge of the overall educational law knowledge base provide a partial answer to the question of how a school administrator can maintain a working familiarity with United States Supreme Court decisions and other important educational law decisions. Another suggestion is to purchase a copy of *A Digest of Supreme Court Decisions Affecting Education* (3rd ed.) by Perry A. Zirkel, Sharon Nalbone Richarardon, and Steven S. Goldberg, or a similar type of publication. *A Digest of Supreme Court Decisions Affecting Education* was conceived by the Phi Delta Kappa Commission on the Impact of Court Decisions on Education, and was first published by the Phi Delta Kappa Educational Foundation in 1978. The third, and most recent, edition was published December 1994. This book provides a written case summary for each United States Supreme Court case that affects education, including cases involving public and private schools and institutions of higher education. Within each summary is information regarding the case citation, the facts, the holding (court's decision), and the basis for the decision.

Another suggestion is to develop your own legal decision-making flow charts. Thirty-three examples of these charts constitute the remaining portion of this chapter. The cases (all United States Supreme Court cases) from which these exemplary charts were developed were selected because of their applicability and utility for those working as administrators at the school level. There are three categories of charts included in the material: cases involving student management problems, instructional program issues, and personnel management concerns. Different from a case summary or legal brief, a legal decision-making flow chart provides a one page visually appealing overview of the case with the content of the chart focusing on that which is most pertinent to administrative decision making.

CONSTRUCTING AND USING LEGAL
DECISION-MAKING FLOW CHARTS

Legal decision-making flow charts (see Figure 5.1) consist of information categorized into three columns. The charts are read from top down and left to right beginning in the upper left-hand column. After reading down the first column, one moves to the top of the second column, repeating the process, and then on to the third column. In the first column, the reader initially encounters a file folder indicating the educational category (i.e., student management, instructional program, or personnel management) and the topic of the flow chart. For example, in Figure 5.1 the words STUDENT MANAGEMENT (which are capitalized) appear and identify the educational category in which the case being considered fits. In parenthesis below the educational category, but still in the folder, is the name of the topic. In this instance, the topic is "search and seizure." The next box provides the name and citation of the case actually under review. The case in this example is *New Jersey v. T.L.O.* The final item in the first column is the issue on which the court was asked to rule.

The second column, as the heading suggests, provides succinct statements of the judicial holding(s), test(s), and/or standard(s) enunciated by the court. An arrow or multiple arrows are drawn for visual effect to show that the holdings, tests, and standards come from the court case under consideration. The summary in each box is followed by a page number which refers to the page of the legal reporter, noted in the case box in column one, where the actual quote or information supporting the paraphrased material can be found. In the *New Jersey v. T.L.O.* case, there are four boxes in the second column. The first box contains the court holding that public school officials are state actors and subject to the Fourth Amendment's prohibition against unreasonable searches and seizures. The second box notes the court holding that school officials need not obtain warrants before searching a student who is under their authority. The third box informs the reader that "reasonable suspicion" is the court-established legal standard that must be met before a principal or other school official may initiate a search of a student or of the

FIGURE 5.1. LEGAL DECISION-MAKING FLOW CHART

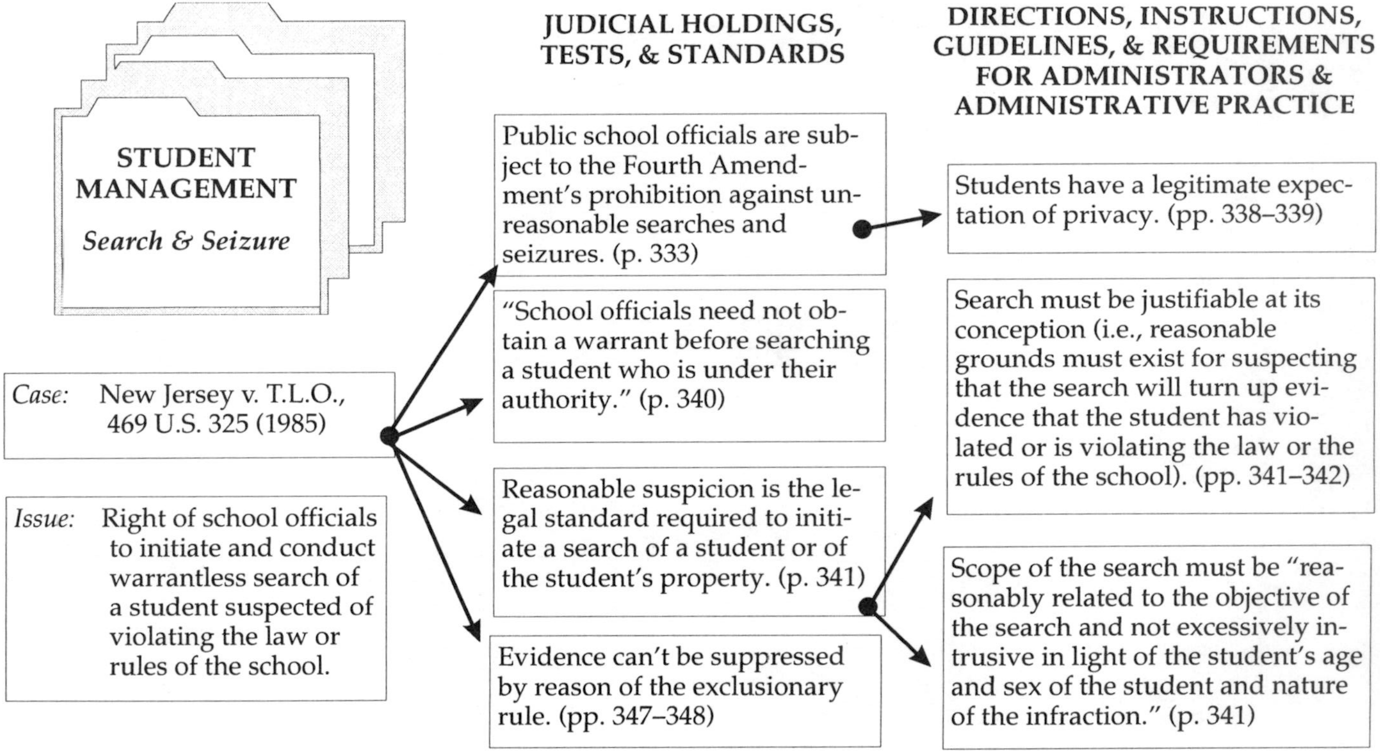

STUDENT MANAGEMENT

Search & Seizure

Case: New Jersey v. T.L.O., 469 U.S. 325 (1985)

Issue: Right of school officials to initiate and conduct warrantless search of a student suspected of violating the law or rules of the school.

JUDICIAL HOLDINGS, TESTS, & STANDARDS

Public school officials are subject to the Fourth Amendment's prohibition against unreasonable searches and seizures. (p. 333)

"School officials need not obtain a warrant before searching a student who is under their authority." (p. 340)

Reasonable suspicion is the legal standard required to initiate a search of a student or of the student's property. (p. 341)

Evidence can't be suppressed by reason of the exclusionary rule. (pp. 347–348)

DIRECTIONS, INSTRUCTIONS, GUIDELINES, & REQUIREMENTS FOR ADMINISTRATORS & ADMINISTRATIVE PRACTICE

Students have a legitimate expectation of privacy. (pp. 338–339)

Search must be justifiable at its conception (i.e., reasonable grounds must exist for suspecting that the search will turn up evidence that the student has violated or is violating the law or the rules of the school). (pp. 341–342)

Scope of the search must be "reasonably related to the objective of the search and not excessively intrusive in light of the student's age and sex of the student and nature of the infraction." (p. 341) student's property. Finally, the fourth or last box indicates that evidence properly obtained without a search warrant in a school context can't be suppressed by reason of the exclusionary rule.

The third column is labeled "Directions, Instructions, Guidelines, and Requirements for Administrators and Administrative Practice." Into this column are placed actual or paraphrased statements from the court's opinion that provide practical guidance and understanding to educational administrators as they seek direction in their decision-making responsibilities. For example, in the *New Jersey v. T.L.O.* case, the first box contains an important guideline that all administrators should remember; namely, that students have a legitimate expectation of privacy. The second and third boxes provide the requirements, instructions, and directions for carrying out a search based on "reasonable suspicion." Arrows again provide a visual connection between relevant material in columns two and three.

One advantage of the decision-making flow charts is the ease with which an administrator can recall the nature of the case. More importantly, the charts provide a summary of the critical holdings, standards, and legal directions that should be followed or considered as one works through the legal decision-making model described in Chapter 4. The concept of legal decision-making flow charts is being introduced as part of this book and is not currently available commercially. However, the author has personally used them in his teaching and has shared them with practicing administrators who have found them very useful in their individual administrative practices. The charts are tools or aids that principals and other school administrators can easily develop themselves and use over and over again to significantly reduce the time that is required in going back numerous times to read a particular court opinion.

The thirty-three charts by category, topic, and case title are:

- ◆ Student Management
    - Suppression of silent expression *(Tinker v. Des Moines Independent Community School District)*

- Disciplining students for offensively lewd and indecent speech (*Bethel School District No. 403 v. Fraser*)
- Censorship of school sponsored student newspaper (*Hazelwood School District v. Kuhlmeier*)
- Legality of the equal access act (*Board of Education of the Westside Community Schools v. Mergens*)
- Search and seizure (*New Jersey v. T.L.O.*)
- Random drug testing of student athletes (*Vernonia School District 47J v. Acton*)
- Corporal punishment (*Ingraham v. Wright*)
- Suspension (*Goss v. Lopez*)
- Discipline of disabled students (*Honig v. Doe*)

♦ Instructional Program

- Released time to attend religious instruction (*Zorach v. Clauson*)
- Prayer in public schools (*Engel v. Vitale*)
- Bible reading and recitation of Lord's Prayer (*School District of Abington v. Schempp*)
- Silent voluntary prayer (*Wallace v. Jaffree*)
- State-sponsored prayer at graduation exercises (*Lee v. Weisman*)
- State monopoly over instruction (*Pierce v. Society of Sisters*)
- Compulsory attendance (*Wisconsin v. Yoder*)
- Compulsory flag salute and pledge of allegiance (*West Virginia State Board of Education v. Barnette*)
- Prohibiting the teaching of foreign languages (*Meyer v. Nebraska*)
- Teaching evolution (*Epperson v. Arkansas*)
- English language instruction for non-English–speaking students (*Lau v. Nichols*)

- Denial of instruction to children of illegal aliens (*Plyler v. Doe*)
- Teaching creation science (*Edwards v. Aguillard*)
- Free appropriate education under the Education of the Handicapped Act (*Board of Education of Hendrick Hudson Central School District v. Rowley*)
- Loaning books to private and parochial schools (*Board of Education of Central School District No. 1 v. Allen*)
- Posting the Ten Commandments on classroom walls (*Stone v. Graham*)
- Removal of books from school libraries (*Board of Education, Island Tree Union Free School District No. 26 v. Pico*)
- Use of school building by religious group during noninstructional time (*Lamb's Chapel v. Center Moriches Union Free District*)

- Personnel Management
  - Right of teachers to speak on public issues (*Pickering v. Board of Education of Township High School District*)
  - Violation of teacher's free speech as a bar to dismissal (*Mt. Healthy City School District Board of Education v. Doyle*)
  - Right to express views privately to employer (*Givhan v. Western Line Consolidated School District*)
  - Personal versus private speech in public employment context (*Connick v. Myers*)
  - Necessity of a hearing in a nonretention action (*Board of Regents of State Colleges v. Roth*)
  - De facto tenure (*Perry v. Sinderman*)

STUDENT MANAGEMENT
Suppression of Silent Expression

Case: Tinker v. Des Moines Independent Community School District, 393 U.S. 503 (1969)

Issue: Pertains to the constitutional right of a public school student to silently and passively express an opinion, unaccompanied by any disorder or disturbance in a public school without threat of prohibition, discipline, or punishment from school officials.

JUDICIAL HOLDINGS, TESTS, & STANDARDS

"First Amendment rights, applied in light of the special characteristics of the school environment, are available to teachers and students. It can hardly be argued that either students or teachers shed their constitutional rights to freedom of speech or expression at the school house gate." (p. 506)

"In order for the state in the person of school officials to justify prohibition of a particular expression of opinion, it must be able to show that its action was caused by something more than a mere desire to avoid the discomfort and unpleasantness that always accompany an unpopular viewpoint. Certainly, where there is no finding and no showing that engaging in the forbidden conduct would 'materially and substantially interfere with the requirements of appropriate discipline in the operation of the school,' the prohibition cannot be sustained." (p. 509)

DIRECTIONS, INSTRUCTIONS, GUIDELINES, & REQUIREMENTS FOR ADMINISTRATORS & ADMINISTRATIVE PRACTICE

"In our system, state-operated schools may not be enclaves of totalitarianism. School officials do not possess absolute authority over their students. Students in school as well as out of school are 'persons' under our Constitution. They are possessed of fundamental rights which the state must respect, just as they themselves must respect their obligations to the state." (p. 511)

"In our system, students may not be regarded as closed-circuit recipients of only that which the state chooses to communicate." (p. 511)

"...undifferentiated fear or apprehension of a disturbance is not enough to overcome the right to freedom of expression." (p. 508)

STUDENT MANAGEMENT

Disciplining Students for Offensively Lewd and Indecent Speech

Case: Bethel School District No. 403 v. Fraser, 478 U.S. 675 (1986)

Issue: Pertains to (1) the constitutionality of public schools to prohibit the use by students of vulgar and offensive terms in public school discourse and (2) the required elements of due process in actions involving school disciplinary rules prohibiting obscene and vulgar language by students in school.

JUDICIAL HOLDINGS, TESTS, & STANDARDS

"A school need not tolerate student speech that is inconsistent with its basic mission." (p. 685)

"...it is a highly appropriate function of public school education to prohibit the use of vulgar and offensive terms in public discourse....Nothing in the Constitution prohibits the states from insisting that certain modes of expression are inappropriate and subject to sanctions." (p. 683)

A school disciplinary rule prescribing "obscene" language together with a prespeech warning by teachers of the inappropriateness of a speech constitutes adequate due process warning that speech might result in sanctions or discipline. (p. 686)

DIRECTIONS, INSTRUCTIONS, GUIDELINES, & REQUIREMENTS FOR ADMINISTRATORS & ADMINISTRATIVE PRACTICE

"The determination of what manner of speech in the classroom or in school assembly is inappropriate properly rests with the school board." (p. 683)

"It does not follow...that simply because the use of an offensive form of expression may not be prohibited to adults making what the speaker considers a political point, the same latitude must be permitted to children in a public school....The constitutional rights of students in public school are not automatically coextensive with the rights of adults in other settings." (p. 682)

"Given [a] school's need to be able to impose disciplinary sanctions for a wide range of unanticipated conduct disruptive of the educational process,...school disciplinary rules need not be as detailed as a criminal code which imposes criminal sanctions." (p. 686)

"Two days' suspension from school does not rise to the level of a penal sanction calling for the full panoply of procedural due process protections applicable to a criminal prosecution." (p. 686)

DIRECTIONS, INSTRUCTIONS, GUIDELINES, & REQUIREMENTS FOR ADMINISTRATORS & ADMINISTRATIVE PRACTICE

"A school...also retain[s] the authority to refuse to sponsor speech that might reasonably be perceived to advocate drug or alcohol use, irresponsible sex, or conduct otherwise inconsistent with 'the shared values of a civilized social order,' or to associate the school with any position other than neutrality on matters of political controversy." (p. 272)

"...a school may in its capacity as publisher of a school newspaper or producer of a school play 'disassociate itself' not only from speech that would 'substantially interfere with [its] work...or impinge upon the rights of other students,' but also from speech that is, for example, ungrammatical, poorly written, inadequately researched, biased or prejudiced, vulgar or profane, or unsuitable for immature audiences." (p. 271)

JUDICIAL HOLDINGS, TESTS, & STANDARDS

"...we hold that educators do not offend the First Amendment by exercising editorial control over the style and content of student speech in school-sponsored expressive activities so long as their actions are reasonably related to legitimate pedagogical concerns." (p. 273)

When censorship has no valid educational purpose, the courts may intervene to protect student's free speech rights. (p. 273)

STUDENT MANAGEMENT

Censorship of School-sponsored Student Newspaper

Case: Hazelwood School District v. Kuhlmeier, 484 U.S. 260 (1988)

Issue: Pertains to the constitutional right of public school officials to exercise editorial control over school-sponsored student publications.

JUDICIAL HOLDINGS, TESTS, & STANDARDS

DIRECTIONS, INSTRUCTIONS, GUIDELINES, & REQUIREMENTS FOR ADMINISTRATORS & ADMINISTRATIVE PRACTICE

STUDENT MANAGEMENT

Legality of the Equal Access Act

Case: Board of Education of the Westside Community Schools v. Mergens, 496 U.S. 226 (1990)

Issue: Pertains to the constitutionality of the congressionally enacted Equal Access Act.*

"Congress' avowed purpose to prevent discrimination against religious and other types of speech—is undeniably secular....Accordingly we hold that the Equal Access Act does not on its face contravene the Establishment Clause." (pp. 249 and 253)

"Unfortunately, the Act does not define the crucial phrase 'noncurriculum related student groups.' Our...task is therefore one of interpretation." (p. 237)

"We think that the term 'noncurriculum related student groups' is best interpreted broadly to mean any student group that does not directly relate to the body of courses offered by the school. In our view, a student group directly relates to a schools curriculum if the subject matter of the group is actually taught, or will be taught, or will soon be taught, in a regularly offered course; if the subject matter of the group concerns the body of courses as a whole; if participation in the group is required for a particular course; or if participation in the group results in academic credit." (pp. 239–240)

* The Equal Access Act reads in part as follows: "It shall be unlawful for any public secondary school which receives Federal financial assistance and which has a limited open forum to deny equal access or a fair opportunity to, or discriminate against, any students who wish to conduct a meeting within that limited open forum on the basis of the religious, political, philosophical, or other content of the speech at such meetings." (20 U.S.C. § 4071 [a]). A limited open forum exists whenever a public secondary school "grants an offering to or opportunity for one or more noncurriculum related student groups to meet on school premises during noninstructional time" (20 U.S.C. § 4071 [b]).

STUDENT MANAGEMENT
Search & Seizure

Case: New Jersey v. T.L.O., 469 U.S. 325 (1985)

Issue: Right of school officials to initiate and conduct warrantless search of a student suspected of violating the law or rules of the school

JUDICIAL HOLDINGS, TESTS, & STANDARDS

Public school officials are subject to the Fourth Amendment's prohibition against unreasonable searches and seizures. (p. 333)

"School officials need not obtain a warrant before searching a student who is under their authority." (p. 340)

Reasonable suspicion is the legal standard required to initiate a search of a student or of the student's property. (p. 341)

Evidence can't be suppressed by reason of the exclusionary rule. (pp. 347–348)

DIRECTIONS, INSTRUCTIONS, GUIDELINES, & REQUIREMENTS FOR ADMINISTRATORS & ADMINISTRATIVE PRACTICE

Students have a legitimate expectation of privacy. (pp. 338–339)

Search must be justifiable at its conception (i.e., reasonable grounds must exist for suspecting that the search will turn up evidence that the student has violated or is violating the law or the rules of the school). (pp. 341–342)

Scope of the search must be "reasonably related to the objective of the search and not excessively intrusive in light of the student's age and sex of the student and nature of the infraction." (p. 341)

JUDICIAL HOLDINGS, TESTS, & STANDARDS

"Taking into account all the factors we have considered —the decreased expectation of privacy, the relative unobtrusiveness of the search, and the severity of the need met by the search —we conclude Vernonia's policy is reasonable and hence constitutional." (p. 2396)

DIRECTIONS, INSTRUCTIONS, GUIDELINES, & REQUIREMENTS FOR ADMINISTRATORS & ADMINISTRATIVE PRACTICE

"We caution against the assumption that suspicionless drug testing will readily pass constitutional muster in other contexts." (p. 2396)

Student athletes have less legitimate privacy expectation due to communal undress, preseason physical exams, rules regulating conduct, and voluntary nature of activity. (See pp. 2392–2393)

Policy in question was viewed as relatively unobtrusive because of process for obtaining samples, what urine was tested for, use of results, and limited range of those having access to information. (See pp. 2393–2394).

A high degree of governmental concern over student drug problems was affirmatively shown to exist.

STUDENT MANAGEMENT

Random Drug Testing of Student Athletes

Case: Vernonia School District 47J v. Acton,* 115 S. Ct. 2386 (1995)

Issue: Pertains to the right of school districts under the Fourth and Fourteenth Amendment to the United States Constitution to establish a random urinalysis drug testing program of students who voluntarily wish to participate in extracurricular athletic programs.

*Actual case involved the legality of a specific school district (Vernonia School District 47J in Oregon) policy which required students to submit to random urinalysis in order to compete in interscholastic sports. The policy was introduced because of the school district's contention that the use of drugs by student athletes had reached "epidemic proportions." Specifically, there had been an increase in the number of disciplinary referrals concerning athletes that school administrators attributed to drugs.

STUDENT MANAGEMENT

Corporal Punishment

Case: Ingraham v. Wright, 430 U.S. 651 (1977)

Issue: Pertains to the constitutionality of corporal punishment as a means of student discipline in public schools.

JUDICIAL HOLDINGS, TESTS, & STANDARDS

The Cruel and Unusual Punishment Clause of the Eighth Amendment to the U. S. Constitution does not apply to disciplinary corporal punishment in public schools. ("...when public school teachers or administrators impose disciplinary corporal punishment, the Eighth Amendment is inapplicable.") (p. 671)

"...we find that corporal punishment in public school implicates a constitutionally protected liberty interest...[the] right to be free from and to obtain judicial relief, for unjustified intrusions on personal security." (pp. 672–673)

"We hold that the traditional common law remedies are fully adequate to afford due process." (p. 672)

DIRECTIONS, INSTRUCTIONS, GUIDELINES, & REQUIREMENTS FOR ADMINISTRATORS & ADMINISTRATIVE PRACTICE

"We conclude that the Due Process Clause does not require notice and hearing prior to the imposition of corporal punishment in the public schools." (p. 682)

"In view of the low incidence of abuse, the openness of our schools, and the common law safeguards that already exist, the risk of error that may result in violation of a school child's substantive rights can only be viewed as minimal." (p. 682)

"Teachers and school authorities are unlikely to inflict corporal punishment unnecessarily or excessively when a possible consequence of doing so is the institution of civil or criminal proceedings against them." (p. 678)

DIRECTIONS, INSTRUCTIONS, GUIDELINES, & REQUIREMENTS FOR ADMINISTRATORS & ADMINISTRATIVE PRACTICE

Generally, "notice and hearing should precede [a] student's removal from school." However, where student's presence endangers persons or property or threatens disruption of the academic process, thus justifying immediate removal, the notice and hearing may follow as soon as practicable. (pp. 582–583)

"There need be no delay between the time notice is given and the time of the hearing." Hearing does not require a formalistic proceeding (i.e., legal counsel, confronting and cross-examining witnesses, calling own witnesses, etc.) (p. 582)

Longer suspensions or expulsions or unusual situations will generally require added procedural protections. (p. 584)

JUDICIAL HOLDINGS, TESTS, & STANDARDS

"A 10-day suspension from school is not *de minimis* in our view and may not be imposed in complete disregard of the Due Process Clause." (p. 576)

"Due Process requires, in connection with a suspension of 10 days or less, that the student be given oral or written notice of the charges against him, and if he denies them, an explanation of the evidence the authorities have and an opportunity to present his side of the story." (p. 581)

STUDENT MANAGEMENT

Suspension

Case: Goss v. Lopez, 419 U.S. 565 (1975)

Issue: Pertains to the necessity of public school officials providing students with Fourteenth Amendment procedural due process protections in conjunction with disciplinary suspension actions.

JUDICIAL HOLDINGS, TESTS, & STANDARDS

DIRECTIONS, INSTRUCTIONS, GUIDELINES, & REQUIREMENTS FOR ADMINISTRATORS & ADMINISTRATIVE PRACTICE

STUDENT MANAGEMENT

Discipline of Disabled Students

Case: Honig v. Doe, 484 U.S. 305 (1988)

Issue: Pertains to the right of public school officials to remove a disabled child, including a seriously emotionally disturbed child, from school for violent and disruptive conduct related to their disabilities despite the child's educational placement under the Education of the Handicapped Act (EHA).

"We think it clear...that Congress very much meant to strip schools of the unilateral authority they had traditionally employed to exclude disabled students, particularly emotionally disturbed students, from school." (p. 323)

"Congress did not leave school administrators powerless to deal with dangerous students." (p. 323)

"Congress passed the EHA after finding that school systems across the country had excluded one out of every eight disabled students from classes." (p. 324)

Interim placements may be made where parents and school officials agree on one. (pp. 324–325)

Normal procedures such as the use of study carrels, timeouts, detention, or restriction of privileges can be used with children who are endangering themselves or others. (p. 325)

"Where a student poses an immediate threat to the safety of others, officials may temporarily suspend him or her for up to 10 school days." (p. 325)

Where parents of a truly dangerous child refuse to permit a change in placement, school officials may seek the assistance of the courts. (p. 326)

DIRECTIONS, INSTRUCTIONS, GUIDELINES, & REQUIREMENTS FOR ADMINISTRATORS & ADMINISTRATIVE PRACTICE

"Government may not finance religious groups nor undertake religious instruction nor blend secular and sectarian education nor use secular institutions to force one or some religion on any person." (p. 314)

States are under no legal obligation to provide release-time programs to accommodate students wishing to attend out-of-school religious instruction.

"...no Constitutional requirement ... makes it necessary for government to be hostile to religion and to throw its weight against efforts to widen the effective scope of religious influence." (p. 314)

JUDICIAL HOLDINGS, TESTS, & STANDARDS

Where "public schools do no more than accommodate their schedules to a program of outside religious instruction" there is no violation of the Establishment Clause of the United State Constitution. (p. 315)

INSTRUCTIONAL PROGRAM

Released Time to Attend Religious Instruction

Case: Zorach v. Clauson, 343 U.S. 306 (1952)

Issue: Pertains to the constitutional right of a state to release public school students, by means of parental request, to leave school buildings and grounds during school time to attend religious instruction and devotion exercises paid for by nonpublic funds.

DIRECTIONS, INSTRUCTIONS, GUIDELINES, & REQUIREMENTS FOR ADMINISTRATORS & ADMINISTRATIVE PRACTICE

JUDICIAL HOLDINGS, TESTS, & STANDARDS

INSTRUCTIONAL PROGRAM

Prayer in Public Schools

The nondenominational character of the prayer and the right to remain silent or to be excused from the classroom during the prayer doesn't alter the court's holding.

"The Constitutional prohibition against laws respecting an establishment of religion... means that in this country it is no part of the business of government to compose official prayers for any group of the American people to recite as a part of a religious program carried on by government." (p. 425)

Case: Engel v. Vitale, 370 U.S. 421 (1962)

Issue: Pertains to the right of a state to compose a denominationally neutral prayer to be recited at the beginning of each school day by those wishing to participate.

DIRECTIONS, INSTRUCTIONS, GUIDELINES, & REQUIREMENTS FOR ADMINISTRATORS & ADMINISTRATIVE PRACTICE

The fact that participation was voluntary and that "no prefatory statements were made, no questions asked or solicited, no comments or explanations made and no interpretations given at or during the exercises" doesn't alter the court's holding. (p. 207)

Nothing in this case precludes the study of the Bible for its literary and historic qualities. (p. 225)

JUDICIAL HOLDINGS, TESTS, & STANDARDS

The practice of requiring that passages be read from the Bible followed by the recitation of the Lord's Prayer each day as a part of a school's curriculum constitutes a state-sponsored religious exercise, which is a violation of the Establishment Clause of the United States Constitution. (p. 223)

INSTRUCTIONAL PROGRAM

Bible Reading and Recitation of Lord's Prayer

Case: School District of Abington Township, Pennsylvania v. Schempp, 374 U.S. 203 (1963)

Issue: Pertains to the constitutional right of a state or local school board to require that passages from the Bible be read or that the Lord's Prayer be recited at the beginning of each school day.

DIRECTIONS, INSTRUCTIONS, GUIDELINES, & REQUIREMENTS FOR ADMINISTRATORS & ADMINISTRATIVE PRACTICE

JUDICIAL HOLDINGS, TESTS, & STANDARDS

INSTRUCTIONAL PROGRAM

Silent Voluntary Prayer

Case: Wallace v. Jaffree, 472 U.S. 38 (1985)

Issue: Pertains to the constitutional right of a state to authorize a one-minute period of silence at the start of each school day for students to engage in meditation or voluntary prayer.

Legislation allowing a one minute moment of silence for the purpose of meditation or voluntary prayer at the beginning of each school day where the express purpose of the statute is to endorse or promote voluntary prayer in school constitutes a state-sponsored religious activity in violation of the Establishment Clause of the United States Constitution. (See pp. 56–61)

The court holding did not pertain to moment of silence statutes whose purpose(s) was something other than expressly promoting in-school voluntary prayer. (See pp. 59 and 62)

DIRECTIONS, INSTRUCTIONS, GUIDELINES, & REQUIREMENTS FOR ADMINISTRATORS & ADMINISTRATIVE PRACTICE

A rule excusing attendance from the graduation does not alter the holding of the court. (p. 595)

Case does not address whether the practice would be acceptable if the "affected citizens are mature adults." (p. 593)

JUDICIAL HOLDINGS, TESTS, & STANDARDS

"The government involvement with religious activity in this case is pervasive, to the point of creating a state-sponsored and state-directed religious exercise in a public school....It is beyond dispute that, at a minimum, the Constitution guarantees that government may not coerce anyone to support or participate in religion or its exercise, or otherwise act in a way which 'establishes a [state] religion or religious faith, or tends to do so.' The State's involvement in the school prayers challenged today violates these central principles." (p. 587)

INSTRUCTIONAL PROGRAM

State-sponsored Prayer at Graduation Exercises

Case: Lee v. Weisman, 505 U.S. 577 (1992)

Issue: Pertains to the constitutionality of permitting school officials to invite clergy to offer a non-sectarian prayer at the beginning and end of a public high school graduation exercise.

DIRECTIONS, INSTRUCTIONS, GUIDELINES, & REQUIREMENTS FOR ADMINISTRATORS & ADMINISTRATIVE PRACTICE

JUDICIAL HOLDINGS, TESTS, & STANDARDS

INSTRUCTIONAL PROGRAM

State Monopoly over Instruction

Case: Pierce v. Society of Sisters, 268 U.S. 510 (1925)

Issue: Pertains to the right of a state to require that all its school age children attend public schools only.

"The fundamental theory of liberty upon which all governments within this Union repose excludes any general power of the state to standardize its children by forcing them to accept instruction from public teachers only." (p. 535)

Ruling does not restrict the state from reasonably "regulating all schools, to inspect, supervise and examine them, their teachers and pupils; to require that all children of proper age attend some school, that teachers shall be of good moral character and patriotic disposition, that certain studies plainly essential to good citizenship must be taught, and that nothing be taught which is manifestly inimical to the public welfare." (p. 534)

DIRECTIONS, INSTRUCTIONS, GUIDELINES, & REQUIREMENTS FOR ADMINISTRATORS & ADMINISTRATIVE PRACTICE

In free exercise claims against compulsory attendance statutes "...it must appear either that the State does not deny the free exercise of religious belief by its requirement, or that there is a state interest of sufficient magnitude to override the interest claiming protection under the Free Exercise Clause." (p. 214)

"A way of life, however virtuous and admirable, may not be interposed as a barrier to reasonable state regulations of education if it is based on purely secular considerations; to have the protection of Religion Clauses, the claims must be rooted in religious belief." (p. 215)

JUDICIAL HOLDINGS, TESTS, & STANDARDS

"A State's interest in universal education, however highly we rank it, is not totally free from a balancing process when it impinges on fundamental rights and interests such as those specifically protected by the Free Exercise Clause of the First Amendment...." (p. 214)

INSTRUCTIONAL PROGRAM

Compulsory Attendance

Case: Wisconsin v. Yoder,* 406 U.S. 205 (1972)

Issue: Pertains to whether a state may require conformance with compulsory attendance laws when such laws impinge upon the Free Exercise of Religion guaranteed under the First Amendment to the United States Constitution.

*Actual case involved the refusal of members of the Old Order Amish religion to send their children to school beyond the eighth grade, believing that high school attendance would endanger their salvation and way of life.

DIRECTIONS, INSTRUCTIONS, GUIDELINES, & REQUIREMENTS FOR ADMINISTRATORS & ADMINISTRATIVE PRACTICE

Although those who brought the case refused to comply on religious grounds, the decision was not based on a religious issue and required no inquiry into the sincerity of their views. (See pp. 634–636)

Holding pertains only to compulsory flag salute and pledge of allegiance. Providing opportunity for voluntary participation in flag salute and pledge of allegiance ceremony was not challenged in the case.

JUDICIAL HOLDINGS, TESTS, & STANDARDS

"We think the action of the local authorities in compelling the flag salute and pledge transcends constitutional limitations on their power and invades the sphere of intellect and spirit which it is the purpose of the First Amendment to our Constitution to reserve from all official control." (p. 642)

"If there is any fixed star in our constitutional constellation, it is that no official, high or petty, can prescribe what shall be orthodox in politics, nationalism, religion or other matters of opinion or force citizens to confess by word or act their faith therein." (p. 642)

INSTRUCTIONAL PROGRAM

Compulsory Flag Salute and Pledge of Allegiance

Case: West Virginia State Board of Education v. Barnette, 319 U.S. 624 (1943)

Issue: Pertains to the constitutional right of a state to *require* as a regular part of the program activities in the public schools that all teachers and pupils salute the flag and repeat the pledge of allegiance or be found insubordinate and subject to disciplinary action.

DIRECTIONS, INSTRUCTIONS,
GUIDELINES, & REQUIREMENTS FOR
ADMINISTRATORS & ADMINISTRATIVE
PRACTICE

JUDICIAL HOLDINGS,
TESTS, & STANDARDS

INSTRUCTIONAL
PROGRAM

*Prohibiting the
Teaching of Foreign
Languages*

Case: Meyer v. Nebraska, 262
U.S. 390 (1923)

Issue: Pertains to the constitutional right of a state to prohibit the teaching in any private, denominational, parochial, or public school, of any modern language, other than English, to any child who has not successfully passed the eighth grade.

Where (as in this case) "no emergency has arisen which renders knowledge by a child of some language other than English so clearly harmful as to justify its inhibition" (p. 403), the act goes beyond the police power of the state and violates the liberty interests of the Fourteenth Amendment of the United States Constitution.

"Mere knowledge of the German language cannot reasonably be regarded as harmful." (p. 400)

"The power of the state to compel attendance at some school and to make reasonable regulations for all schools, including a requirement that they shall give instructions in English, is not questioned." (p. 402)

DIRECTIONS, INSTRUCTIONS, GUIDELINES, & REQUIREMENTS FOR ADMINISTRATORS & ADMINISTRATIVE PRACTICE

"Government in our democracy, state and national, must be neutral in matters of religious theory, doctrine, and practice. It may not be hostile to any religion or the advocacy of no-religion; and it may not aid, foster, or promote one religion, or religious theory against another or even against the militant opposite." (pp. 103–104)

The right of a state to prescribe the public school curriculum does not include the right to prohibit the teaching of a theory or doctrine for reasons that are contrary to the Establishment Clause of the United States Constitution. (p. 107)

JUDICIAL HOLDINGS, TESTS, & STANDARDS

Where the sole reason for banning the teaching of evolution is that a particular religious group considers the theory to conflict with their religious beliefs, the banning constitutes a violation of the Establishment Clause of the United States Constitution. (See pp. 107–109)

INSTRUCTIONAL PROGRAM

Teaching Evolution

Case: Epperson v. Arkansas, 393 U.S. 97 (1968)

Issue: Pertains to the right of a state for religious reasons to exclude from its curriculum the teaching of the theory that man evolved from other species of life (evolution).

DIRECTIONS, INSTRUCTIONS, GUIDELINES, & REQUIREMENTS FOR ADMINISTRATORS & ADMINISTRATIVE PRACTICE

JUDICIAL HOLDINGS, TESTS, & STANDARDS

INSTRUCTIONAL PROGRAM

English Language Instruction for Non-English-Speaking Students

Case: Lau v. Nichols, 414 U.S. 563 (1974)

Issue: Pertains to the necessity of public schools under the federal Civil Rights Act of 1964 to provide English language instruction or other adequate instructional procedures to students who do not speak English.

A meaningful opportunity to participate in public education is denied those who can't speak English when the basic language of instruction is English and no English instruction is provided such students. It also follows that such a practice violates the Civil Rights Act of 1964 which bans discrimination based "on the grounds of race, color, or national origin" in "any program receiving federal financial assistance." Various implementing regulations are also violated. (pp. 565–569)

"Basic skills are at the very core of what...public schools teach. Imposition of a requirement that, before a child can effectively participate in the educational program, he must already have acquired those basic skills is to make a mockery of public education." (p. 566)

DIRECTIONS, INSTRUCTIONS, GUIDELINES, & REQUIREMENTS FOR ADMINISTRATORS & ADMINISTRATIVE PRACTICE

State interest of

1. Stemming tide of increasing numbers of illegal aliens;
2. Reducing financial burden on high quality public education; and
3. Loosing those educated to productive social or political use because of unlawful presence

are "insubstantial in light of the costs involved to these children." (p. 230)

JUDICIAL HOLDINGS, TESTS, & STANDARDS

The Fourteenth Amendment to the United States Constitution provides that "no state shall…deny to any person within its jurisdiction the equal protection of the laws" and "whatever one's status under the immigration laws, an alien is surely a 'person' in any ordinary sense of that term." (p. 210)

"If [a] state is to deny a discrete group of innocent children the free public education that it offers to other children residing within its borders, that denial must be justified by a showing that it furthers some substantial state interest." (p. 230)

INSTRUCTIONAL PROGRAM

Denial of Instruction to Children of Illegal Aliens

Case: Plyler v. Doe, 457 U.S. 202 (1982)

Issue: Pertains to the constitutionality under the Equal Protection Clause of the Fourteenth Amendment to the United States Constitution of whether a state "may deny undocumented school-age children the free education that it provides to children who are citizens of the United States or legally admitted aliens." (p. 205)

DIRECTIONS, INSTRUCTIONS, GUIDELINES, & REQUIREMENTS FOR ADMINISTRATORS & ADMINISTRATIVE PRACTICE

JUDICIAL HOLDINGS, TESTS, & STANDARDS

INSTRUCTIONAL PROGRAM

Teaching Creation Science

Case: Edwards v. Aguillard, 482 U.S. 578 (1987)

Issue: Pertains to the constitutionality of a state statute forbidding the teaching of the theory of evolution in public schools unless accompanied by instruction in creation science.

"Because the primary purpose of the Creationism Act is to advance a particular religious belief, the Act endorses religion in violation of the First Amendment" to the United States Constitution. (p. 593)

"The...Creationism Act advances a religious doctrine by requiring either the banishment of the theory of evolution from the public school classroom or the presentation of a religious viewpoint that rejects evolution in its entirety." (p. 597)

"...teaching a variety of scientific theories about the origins of humankind to school children might be validly done with the clear secular intent of enhancing the effectiveness of science instruction." (p. 594)

INSTRUCTIONAL PROGRAM

Free Appropriate Education under Education of the Handicapped Act

Case: Board of Education of the Hendrick Hudson Central School District v. Rowley, 458 U.S. 176 (1982)

Issue: Pertains to the interpretation that should be given the "free appropriate public education" provision of the federal Education of the Handicapped Act.

JUDICIAL HOLDINGS, TESTS, & STANDARDS

"Insofar as a state is required to provide a handicapped child with a 'free appropriate public education,' we hold that it satisfies this requirement by providing personalized instruction with sufficient support services to permit the child to benefit educationally from that instruction. Such instruction and services must be provided at public expense, must meet the state's educational standards, must approximate the grade levels used in the state's regular education, and must comport with the child's IEP. In addition, the IEP, and therefore the personalized instruction, should be formulated in accordance with the requirements of the Act, and if the child is being educated in the regular classroom of the public education system, should be reasonably calculated to enable the child to achieve passing marks and advance from grade to grade." (pp. 203–204)

DIRECTIONS, INSTRUCTIONS, GUIDELINES, & REQUIREMENTS FOR ADMINISTRATORS & ADMINISTRATIVE PRACTICE

"...furnishing handicapped children with only such services as are available to nonhandicapped children would in all probability fall short of the statutory requirement of 'free appropriate public education;' to require on the other hand, the furnishing of every special service necessary to maximize each handicapped child's potential is, we think, further than Congress intended to go." (pp. 198–199)

INSTRUCTIONAL PROGRAM

Loaning Books to Private and Parochial Schools

Case: Board of Education of Central School District No. 1 v. Allen, Commissioner of Education of New York, 392 U.S. 236 (1968)

Issue: Pertains to the constitutionality of a state statute requiring local public school authorities to lend textbooks free of charge to all students in grades 7 to 12, including those in private and parochial schools.

JUDICIAL HOLDINGS, TESTS, & STANDARDS

Where the purpose and effect of the statute is the furtherance of secular educational opportunities for students, it does not violate the Establishment Clause of the First Amendment to the United States Constitution. (pp. 243–244)

DIRECTIONS, INSTRUCTIONS, GUIDELINES, & REQUIREMENTS FOR ADMINISTRATORS & ADMINISTRATIVE PRACTICE

Statute did "not authorize the loaning of religious books, and the State claimed no right to distribute religious literature." (p. 244)

"Books are furnished at the request of the pupil and ownership remains, at least technically, in the state. Thus, no funds or books are furnished to parochial schools, and the financial benefit is to parents and children, not to schools." (pp. 243–244)

DIRECTIONS, INSTRUCTIONS, GUIDELINES, & REQUIREMENTS FOR ADMINISTRATORS & ADMINISTRATIVE PRACTICE

"It does not matter that the posted copies of the Ten Commandments are financed by voluntary private contributions...." (p. 42)

That the secular application of the Ten Commandments has been adopted as the fundamental legal code of Western civilization and common law of the United States made no difference to the court because, in the view of the court, the statutes preeminent purpose was "plainly religious in nature." (p. 41)

JUDICIAL HOLDINGS, TESTS, & STANDARDS

"...statute requiring the posting of the Ten Commandments in public school rooms has no secular legislative purpose, and is therefore unconstitutional." (p. 41)

INSTRUCTIONAL PROGRAM

Posting the Ten Commandments on Classroom Walls

Case: Stone v. Graham, 449 U.S. 39 (1980)

Issue: Pertains to the constitutionality of a state statute requiring the posting of a copy of the Ten Commandments on the wall of each public school classroom.

INSTRUCTIONAL PROGRAM

Removal of Books from School Libraries

Case: Board of Education, Island Trees Union Free School District No. 26 v. Pico, 457 U.S. 853 (1982)

Issue: Pertains to whether the First Amendment to the United States Constitution imposes limitations on the discretionary authority of local school board members to remove books from secondary school libraries.

JUDICIAL HOLDINGS, TESTS, & STANDARDS

"...We hold that local school boards may not remove books from school library shelves simply because they dislike the ideas contained in those books and seek by their removal to 'prescribe what shall be orthodox in politics, nationalism, or other matters of opinion.'" (p. 872)

Boards "rightly possess significant discretion to determine the content of their school libraries. But that discretion may not be exercised in a narrowly partisan or political manner." (p. 870)

DIRECTIONS, INSTRUCTIONS, GUIDELINES, & REQUIREMENTS FOR ADMINISTRATORS & ADMINISTRATIVE PRACTICE

"...an unconstitutional motivation would not be demonstrated if it were shown that petitioners had decided to remove the books at issue because they were pervasively vulgar." (p. 871)

"...if it were demonstrated that the removal decision was based solely upon the 'educational suitability' of the books in question, then their removal would be perfectly permissible.'" (p. 871)

"...nothing in our decision today affects in any way the discretion of a local board to choose to *add* to the libraries of their school. Because we are concerned in this case with the suppression of ideas, our holding today affects only the discretion to *remove* books." (pp. 871–872)

DIRECTIONS, INSTRUCTIONS, GUIDELINES, & REQUIREMENTS FOR ADMINISTRATORS & ADMINISTRATIVE PRACTICE

Unless expressly required by state law, school districts need not permit after-hour use of its property. "There is no question that the District, like the private owner of property, may legally preserve the property under its control for the use to which it is dedicated." (pp. 390–391)

JUDICIAL HOLDINGS, TESTS, & STANDARDS

Denial of presentation violates Freedom of Speech under the First Amendment to the United States Constitution because it discriminates on the basis of viewpoint by permitting school facilities to be used for the presentation of all views about family issues and child rearing except those addressing the subject from a religious point of view. ("'…the government violates the First Amendment when it denies access to a speaker solely to suppress the point of view he espouses on an otherwise includible subject.'" [p. 394])

INSTRUCTIONAL PROGRAM

Use of School Building by Religious Group During Noninstructional Time

Case: Lamb's Chapel v. Center Moriches Union Free District, 508 U.S. 385 (1993)

Issue: Pertains to the constitutionality of permitting school property to be used during noninstructional time for the presentation of views about family issues and child rearing except those dealing with the subject from a religious point of view where state law allows use of building for social, civic, and recreational uses but prohibits use by any group for religious purposes.

PERSONNEL MANAGEMENT

Right of Teachers to Speak on Public Issues

Case: Pickering v. Board of Education of Township High School District 205, 391 U.S. 563 (1968)

Issue: Pertains to the constitutional right of public school teachers to speak on public issues.

JUDICIAL HOLDINGS, TESTS, & STANDARDS

Public employees do not relinquish the First Amendment right of free speech to comment on matters of public interest by reason of government employment.

A balance must be struck "between the interests of the teacher, as a citizen, in commenting on matters of public concern and the interest of the state, as an employer, in promoting the efficiency of the public services it performs through its employees." (p. 568)

"...absent proof of false statements knowingly or recklessly made by him, a teacher's exercise of his right to speak on issues of public importance may not furnish the basis for his dismissal from public employment." (p. 574)

DIRECTIONS, INSTRUCTIONS, GUIDELINES, & REQUIREMENTS FOR ADMINISTRATORS & ADMINISTRATIVE PRACTICE

"[The] Pickering Balance as it has come to be known, looks to the following factors: (1) the need for harmony in the office or work place; (2) whether the government's responsibilities require a close working relationship to exist between the plaintiff and co-workers when the speech in question has caused or could cause the relationship to deteriorate; (3) the time, manner, and place of the speech; (4) the context in which the speech arose; (5) the degree of public interest in the speech; and (6) whether the speech impeded the employee's ability to perform his or her duties." (See Roberts v. Van Buren Public Schools, 773 F. 2d 949 (8th Cir. 1985))

DIRECTIONS, INSTRUCTIONS, GUIDELINES, & REQUIREMENTS FOR ADMINISTRATORS & ADMINISTRATIVE PRACTICE

"The constitutional principle at stake is sufficiently vindicated if such an employee is placed in no worse a position than if he had not engaged in the conduct. A borderline or marginal candidate should not have the employment question resolved against him because of constitutionally protected conduct. But that same candidate ought not to be able, by engaging in such conduct, to prevent his employer from assessing his performance record and reaching a decision not to hire on the basis of that record, simply because the protected conduct makes the employer more certain of the correctness of its decision." (pp. 285–286)

JUDICIAL HOLDINGS, TESTS, & STANDARDS

If in the absence of the protected conduct a preponderance of evidence would have reached the decision to dismiss, the dismissal action is valid. (See p. 287)

PERSONNEL MANAGEMENT

Violation of Teacher's Free Speech as a Bar to Dismissal

Case: Mt. Healthy City School District Board of Education v. Doyle, 429 U.S. 274 (1977)

Issue: Pertains to whether a teacher may be dismissed even if a "nonpermissible reason, e.g., exercise of First Amendment rights, played a substantial part in the decision" to dismiss. (p. 284)

DIRECTIONS, INSTRUCTIONS,
GUIDELINES, & REQUIREMENTS FOR
ADMINISTRATORS & ADMINISTRATIVE
PRACTICE

"Having opened his office door to petitioner, the principal was hardly in a position to argue that he was the unwilling recipient of her views." (p. 415)

Teacher had made demands on but two occasions and those demands were viewed as neither petty nor unreasonable. (See pp. 412–413)

JUDICIAL HOLDINGS,
TESTS, & STANDARDS

"The First Amendment forbids abridgement of the 'freedom of speech.' Neither the Amendment itself nor our decisions indicate that this freedom is lost to the public employee who arranges to communicate privately with his employer rather than to spread his views before the public." (pp. 415–416)

PERSONNEL
MANAGEMENT

*Right to Express
Views Privately to
Employer*

Case: Givhan v. Western Line Consolidated School District, 439 U.S. 410 (1979)

Issue: Pertains to the constitutional right of a public employee to express his/her views on a matter of public interest privately to his/her employer rather than to do so publicly.*

* In the actual case the employee, a teacher, had criticized the policies and practices of the employing school district and the federal district court had concluded that those comments were the primary reason for the district's failure to renew her teaching contract.

JUDICIAL HOLDINGS, TESTS, & STANDARDS

In determining the free speech rights of a public employee, the task is as noted in *Pickering*, to seek "a balance between the interests of the [employee], as a citizen, in commenting upon matters of public concern and the interest of the State, as an employer, in promoting the efficiency of the public services it performs through its employees." (See p. 142)

"When employee expression cannot be fairly considered as relating to any matter of political, social, or other concern to the community, government officials should enjoy wide latitude in managing their offices, without intrusive oversight by the judiciary in the name of the "First Amendment." (p. 137)

"While as a matter of good judgment, public officials should be receptive to constructive criticism offered by their employees, the First Amendment does not require a public office to be run as a roundtable for employee complaints over internal office affairs." (p. 149)

DIRECTIONS, INSTRUCTIONS, GUIDELINES, & REQUIREMENTS FOR ADMINISTRATORS & ADMINISTRATIVE PRACTICE

"Whether an employee's speech addresses a matter of public concern must be determined by content, form, and context of a given statement, as revealed by the whole record." (pp. 147–148)

When dismissal from government employment is not based on protective speech, violates no fixed tenure, applicable statute, or regulation, it is not subject to court examination even if the "reasons for dismissal are alleged to be mistaken or unreasonable." (See pp. 146–147)

"...the Government, as an employer, must have wide discretion and control over the management of its personnel and internal affairs. This includes the prerogative to remove employees whose conduct hinders efficient operations and to do so with dispatch. Prolonged retention of a disruptive or otherwise unsatisfactory employee can adversely affect discipline and morale in the workplace, foster disharmony, and ultimately impair the efficiency of an office or agency.'" (p. 151; quote from *Arnett v. Kennedy*, 416 U.S. 134, 168 (1974))

PERSONNEL MANAGEMENT
Personal versus Private Speech in Public Employment Context

Case: Connick v. Myers, 461 U.S. 138 (1983)

Issue: Pertains to the constitutional protection afforded a public employee who speaks out on matters of personal concern.

DIRECTIONS, INSTRUCTIONS, GUIDELINES, & REQUIREMENTS FOR ADMINISTRATORS & ADMINISTRATIVE PRACTICE

Absent charges against a teacher that would place his/her "good name, reputation, honor, or integrity" at stake, there is no liberty interest violated. (See p. 573)

"To have a property interest in a benefit, a person clearly must have more than an abstract need or desire for it. He must have more than a unilateral expectation of it. He must, instead, have a legitimate claim of entitlement to it." (p. 577)

Ruling pertains to reemployment at the end of a contract period and not dismissal for cause during contract period.

Ruling assumes no statutory requirement that reasons be given for nonretention decision.

JUDICIAL HOLDINGS, TESTS, & STANDARDS

The Fourteenth Amendment to the United States Constitution does not require a hearing before the nonrenewal of a nontenured teacher's contract unless the teacher can demonstrate that the decision not to rehire deprived him of a liberty interest or that he had a property interest in continued employment.

PERSONNEL MANAGEMENT
Necessity of a Hearing in a Nonretention Action

Case: Board of Regents of State Colleges v. Roth, 408 U.S. 564 (1972)

Issue: Pertains to the Fourteenth Amendment procedural due process protections guaranteed a teacher in a nonretention action.

DIRECTIONS, INSTRUCTIONS, GUIDELINES, & REQUIREMENTS FOR ADMINISTRATORS & ADMINISTRATIVE PRACTICE

"A written contract with an explicit tenure provision clearly is evidence of a formal understanding that supports a teacher's claim of entitlement to continual employment." (p. 601)

An implied right to continuing employment (de facto tenure) might be shown through the "policies and practices of an institution." (See pp. 602–603)

JUDICIAL HOLDINGS, TESTS, & STANDARDS

"We have made it clear that property interests subject to procedural due process protection are not limited by a few rigid, technical forms. Rather, property denotes a broad range of interests that are secured by 'existing rules or understandings.' A person's interest in a benefit is a 'property' interest for due process purposes if there are such rules or mutually explicit understandings that support [a] claim of entitlement to the benefit." (p. 601)

PERSONNEL MANAGEMENT

De Facto Tenure

Case: Perry v. Sinderman, 408 U.S. 593 (1972)

Issue: Pertains to whether a showing of de facto tenure by a teacher provides a Fourteenth Amendment right to a hearing which requires that the reasons for a nonretention action be put forward and the teacher given an opportunity to challenge and defend against them.

SUGGESTED ACTIVITY

♦ Identify some critical educational law state court cases, or cases decided by federal district or appellate courts in your state, and develop some legal decision-making flow charts of your own.

REFERENCES

Zirkel, P.A., S.N. Richardson, and S.S. Goldberg. (1994). *A Digest of Supreme Court Decisions Affecting Education* (3rd ed.). Bloomington, IN: Phi Delta Kappa Educational Foundation.

6

A PREVENTATIVE APPROACH: FOUR USEFUL IDEAS

There are many excellent tools and techniques that have been developed by school administrators, lawyers, insurance companies, interested professors, and risk management offices, which are designed to assist the practicing school administrator reduce the potential for liability in his/her school or school district. Utilizing these innovations can save time, money, and unnecessary duplication of effort, and can significantly decrease the likelihood of legal action against the school or school district. They can also reduce injuries and make the school a safer and healthier place in which to work or attend. In addition, they can contribute to the confidence and ability of school officials to effectively provide leadership in a legal and regulatory environment. Principals and other school officials should always be on the lookout for ideas they think will help reduce liability and prevent or eliminate legal problems and injury. This chapter presents four simple, yet representative, ideas.

The first two ideas are borrowed (with permission) from the Granite School District situated in the state of Utah. With approximately 80,000 students, this district is the largest school district in the Utah and one of the 40 largest in the United States. Its ideas are *Good Practices* and *A Principal's Monthly School Inspection Report*. The third idea comes from *West's Education Law Reporter* and is the collection and use of *Education Law into Practice* materials. The last idea is the use of materials from legal form books. Several commercial publishers market these books, and copies are available in most law libraries.

GOOD PRACTICES

In the late 1980s, officials in the Granite School District came up with the concept of developing a book they labeled as *Good Practices*. The book, which is really a three-ring binder issued to all school principals, contains one-page statements that detail in a model-like manner how to best execute an administrative act or practice that ordinarily has significant legal and regulatory implications. Any administrator or group of administrators in the district can develop a "good practice" statement and submit it for possible inclusion in the book. Newly proposed statements are reviewed and approved by a committee composed of district-level school services administrators. Approved statements are sent out immediately to all school principals. In August of each year, during a school principals meeting, a new index is distributed and all statements are reviewed. Those wishing to develop a new "good practice" statement or those who are requested to develop and share a "good practice" are instructed to try and keep the length of the statement to a single written page. Eight criterion or tests have been developed, which form the basis on which any submitted "good practice" statement is judged for inclusion in the book:

- ◆ Provides timely notice and opportunity for feedback.
- ◆ Is reasonably related to the orderly, efficient, and safe operation of the school.

- Provides for a fair investigation of allegations or concerns.
- Provides an appeals procedure.
- Recommends that counsel is sought when dealing with difficult issues.
- Insures due process.
- Must not conflict with:
  - Board policy.
  - State or local laws.
  - Administrative memoranda.
  - Professional agreement.
- Avoids practice that may be seen as unreasonable, unfair, or petty.

Fifteen examples from Granite School District's current version of *Good Practices* are used as examples in this book. The titles of these examples are:

- Age of School Entry
- Arrest of Employee
- Athletics
- Building Inspections
- Building Rental
- Films and Videos
- In-School Suspension
- Managing a Teacher Walkout (Elementary)
- Procedures—School Closure
- Record Retention Schedule
- Safe Schools
- Schoolwide Discipline Plan (Elementary)
- Student Travel
- Surplus Teachers
- Selection Committees/Personnel

Granite School District   **Age of School Entry**
School Services

Good Practice
Age of School Entry

Utah law, section 53A-3-402 indicates students entering school must be at least five years of age before September 2 of the year in which admission is sought. Interpretation of the law suggests that a child who is eligible to enter may be placed in any grade for which they have the skills to succeed.

In Granite School District, we recommend that an entering five-year-old be placed in kindergarten and then be evaluated to determine if another grade placement would be more appropriate. The following steps should be followed:

♦ The child should be placed in the kindergarten classroom in order for the teacher to have time with the student. He/she should evaluate the student academically and socially.

♦ Social, emotional, and academic readiness should be evaluated.

♦ A meeting should be held involving team member(s), teacher(s), parent(s), and administrator to review all pertinent information.

♦ A school-eligible child may be enrolled in any grade for which the child is adequately prepared in the opinion of **authorized representatives of the district.**

♦ Evaluation meetings should be done in a timely manner.

Suggestions: A good measure to help in the evaluation process is to place the student in a kindergarten session for half a day and then in the first grade the other half. This will help determine if the student is academically and socially capable of a first grade placement.

Recommended measures to test readiness for moving kindergarten students into first grade:

Lights Retention Scale
Woodcock Johnson 11
Test of Kindergarten/First Grade Readiness Skills

Testing should be completed by a staff member from Student Support Services.

Granite School District   **Athletics**
School Services

Good Practice
Interscholastic Athletic Program Health
Examination and Consent Form

1. All students who participate in interscholastic athletic programs are required to have a physical examination and complete **FORM A** annually.
2. Students are required to show evidence of health/accident insurance coverage for eligibility to participate in interscholastic athletic program.
3. Each secondary school will conduct an annual "Interscholastic Athletic Participation Program." Content should include:
   a. Show and discuss the video: "Warning: it Can Happen to You."
   b. Orientation to the school athletic program.
   c. Parent/athlete meeting with coaches.
   d. Other as deemed necessary.

Granite School District   **Arrest of an Employee**
School Services

Good Practice
Corrective Discipline: Arrest of an Employee

I.   School Services notified that an employee has been arrested
     (Utah Code 77-26-22)
II   Preliminary Response
     A. Conduct preliminary investigation (Superintendency or
         Personnel)
         1. Schedule conference with employee
         2. Employee given the opportunity to explain situation
            and extenuating circumstances, if any
     B. If further consideration is judged necessary, case is re-
         ferred to ASK* Committee.
         1. All documented evidence is reviewed by the ASK
            Committee with consideration given to:
            a. What facts are known regarding the charges?
            b. What standards of conduct are alleged to have
               been violated? (Board Policy V, Section 3, p. 519)
            c. What is the impact of this behavior on students,
               teachers, classified staff, community and par-
               ents? —program needs —student safety —public
               trust
            d. What complaints or concerns have risen from co-
               workers, faculty, the community, the administra-
               tion, students and parents? (Notoriety of
               Conduct)
            e. What, if any, extenuating or aggravating circum-
               stances surround the incident?
            f. What motive for conduct, if any, has the employee
               offered for this conduct?
            g. Is this an isolated incident or a pattern? What is the
               past record for this employee —as a teacher?
               —length of service? —police record? —prior
               help given?
            h. What is the likelihood that this behavior could be
               repeated?
            i. What is the appropriate timeliness of possible fu-
               ture action?

j. What is the balance of "Inhibiting Effect?" (contractual rights of employee involved balanced against rights of people who are harmed by the conduct)

k. What legal precedents must influence a possible course of action?

2. Case is reviewed, possible courses of action are considered (Board Policy V, Sec. 7-12, pp. 521–27)
   a. Letter of warning or reprimand
   b. Suspension without pay
   c. Administrative transfer
   d. Immediate dismissal
   e. Other

3. Preliminary course of action developed by ASK Committee is implemented

III. Continuing Response

A. Disposition of arrest is received (Granite Police).
(indictment, dismissal, pleas bargain, guilty pleas, no contest, etc.)

B. All prior information from II.B.1. above, along with any new information is reviewed and considered by the ASK Committee.

C. Recommendation formulated by the ASK Committee (see II.B.#. above)

D. Recommendation is reviewed by district counsel.

E. Final recommendation is presented to Deputy Superintendent for action.

(*District-coined acronym for Administrative Support Committee. The district has both an elementary and secondary ASK Committee. Members include high-level central office officials from various departments such as Human Resources and School Support Services as well as the district's legal compliance officer.)

Granite School District   **Building Inspections**
School Services   **Maintenance**
                                                Capital Outlay

Good Practice
Building Inspections

Occasionally, your campus will be inspected by various agencies, including the City/County Health Department, the Granite School District Insurance carrier, the State Fire Marshall, the local Fire Marshall, and/or the State Risk Management Office. Following these inspections, you generally receive a letter identifying all of the changes that are recommended to be completed so the building/campus will comply with regulations. Before you send a copy of that letter to your school services supervisor, please review each item and assign it to one of the following categories:

1. C.—The custodial staff will solve this problem.
2. W.O.—A work order will be submitted to maintenance.
3. C.O.—This item will be requested on capital for next year.
4. L.S.—This is an emergency life-safety item and should be resolved as soon as possible.

Mark each item on the letter with the appropriate code: C., W.O., C.O., or L.S. Keep the original copy of the letter and send a copy to School Services. We will work with the capital committee to resolve the immediate life-safety (L.S.) problems.

Granite School District	Rentals
High School Services	Buildings & Grounds

Good Practice
Building & Grounds Rental

1. References:
   a. Utah Code 53A-3-413, -414, and 76-10-106-(3)-(a)
   b. Board Policy IX A- 1
   c. Administrative Memorandum 42
   d. Form—Request for School Facilities
   e. Form—Green Card (GSD Facility Use Permit)

2. Principal or designated administrator: Determine what the applicant wants:
   a. Date, Day, Times
   b. Use, Activity
   c. Space Required (Classroom, Auditorium, Field, etc.)
   d. Equipment, Furniture

3. Provide equitable distribution of school's facilities among community and private applicants.

4. Review policies with the applicant
   a. Rental Fees, Personnel, Insurance
   b. Smoking, Food Sale, etc.
   c. Rental Form (front & back), Green Card (front & back)

5. Review costs and payment with the applicant
   a. Total cost
   b. Deposit
   c. When balance is due

6. Give applicant "Request for Use of School Facilities." Explain that it must be typewritten. Completed form must be submitted in time for school and district approvals.

7. Send completed application to School Services Administrators. *Exception:* For free grounds use send white and green copy only with attached grounds map.

8. Make corrections in final amount due, collect balance, and send to accounting with green copy.

9. Any exceptions (e.g., class reunions) must be approved by the Superintendency.

Granite School District   **Student Discipline**
School Services

Good Practice

Use of In-School Suspension

References: *Administrative memoranda 17.61.101 Board Policy IX.D.9*

NOTE: In-School Suspension (ISS) is an intervention designed to be administered by the principal and used only in severe cases.

1. The principles underlying the In-School Suspension technique are that:

   a. Out-of school suspension has generally not been found to be very effective in reducing incidents of misbehavior.

   b. The **positive reinforcement** that students need and want is available in the classroom.

   c. Persistent misbehavior results in the removal of that positive reinforcement.

2. Use of In-School Suspension (ISS)

   a. Room must be well ventilated and well lighted

   - Media center
   - Resource room at noon
   - Empty classroom
   - Classrooms in other grades
   - Conference room
   - Stage
   - Office

   b. Room must be monitored by principal, teacher, or responsible adult in a matter-of-fact style

   c. Parents must be notified that a student received ISS

   d. Students must not be left alone

   e. Use of ISS must be documented (name, date, infraction, duration)

   f. Students may do school work
   - From a file maintained in the office
   - From classroom assignments

g. ISS rules:
  ♦ No talking to other students
  ♦ Stay in your seat
  ♦ Work on your school work
  ♦ No sleeping
h. Infractions of ISS rules may mean additional time added to ISS
i. Amount of time in ISS may be systematically increased for each subsequent infraction

3. When the use of ISS or the office becomes excessive, it is a signal that the schoolwide plan or an individual classroom plan is not working as effectively as it should.

4. Due Proess including a rudimentary review procedure must be maintained throughout any schoolwide discipline program.

Granite School District   **Teacher Walkout**
High School Services

Good Practice
Managing a Teacher Walkout in Elementary Schools

CASE A: Teachers walk out after school has started

1. Notify a School Services Administrator

2. Make every attempt to keep school open as long as possible.
    a. Double-up classes
    b. Large group activities
    c. Use of aides and PTA volunteers
    d. Use of district subs (if available)

3. Note which teachers walked out and document the amount of time missed on payroll sheets (to the nearest tenth of a day)

4. If you determine that school can no longer be held safely, call a School Services Administrator to recommend early closure.

    a. Recommendation is forwarded to the Superintendency for the action. School Services will notify the principal, the media, Transportation Department, Information Services, and Food Services.
    b. If it is decided to close the school, **do not** make a general announcement to the student body.
    c. Initiate a procedure to find safe transportation home for the students.

        Suggested Means:
        ♦ Calling parents at home/work
        ♦ PTA calling tree
        ♦ Use of neighbors phones
        ♦ District busses

Specific Cautions:

- Do not release students to strangers (see registration cards)
- Be sure students can get in their houses
- Keep students whose safe transport cannot be arranged
- Determine if special safeguards are needed for handicapped cluster units

5. If teachers walk out during elementary planning time, keep track of which teachers have left and record a .2 salary deduction on their payroll sheet.

6. Work with your PTA Board to establish a contingency plan for an orderly school closure.

CASE B: Teachers vote to walk out on the next school day

1. Notify a School Services Administrator

2. A recommendation may be forwarded to the Superintendency for action. If school is to be closed, School Services will notify the principal, the media, Transportation Department, Information Services, and Food Services.

3. Keep an accurate roll for payroll purposes of which teachers came to work.

4. Keep School Services informed as events progress—NO SURPRISES!

Granite School District   **Films and Videos**
School Services

Good Practice
Use of Films and Videos in Educational Settings

Use of Commercially Obtained Video Programs:

Films/videos obtained from video rental stores CANNOT be shown in schools. This is because the written contract that accompanies each rental specifically states that videos rented will NOT be used for public performance, nor for any use, other than home viewing. Therefore, *the use of rented videos in schools is strictly prohibited.*

Purchased videos can be used for "face-to-face" instruction IF a direct connection can be established between the content of the film/video and the instructional objectives found in the state Core Curriculum and/or the district's Blueprint for Learning. It is good practice for you to require each teacher to log "face-to-face" video usage with you and provide copies of lesson plans that include a written assignment, worksheet or evaluation component.

Guidelines for Purchasing videos with School Monies:

When purchasing videos for use in educational settings make certain that: (1) the content of the video directly correlates with the State Core Curriculum and/or the district's Blueprint for Learning, (2) the teacher using the video provides evidence of a lesson plan, worksheet, activity, or evaluative tool to demonstrate a direct link to state/district educational objectives, (3) you indicate on the requisition or purchase order that "this film/video is being purchased for public display in an educational setting", and *(4) films/videos purchased by schools can NEVER be shown for entertainment, motivation, or reward purposes unless public performance rights have been obtained.*

Selection and Viewing of Films and Videos:

Granite School District does not allow for the showing of "R" or "X" rated materials. Use of materials with "PG" or "PG-13" ratings are left up to the approval of the principal.

Ratings of films and videos in the "PG" or "PG-13" categories contain at least one of the following: violence, profanity, sexual innuendo, partial nudity. Before showing such a film or video, send home a note stating the rating and cause for the rating. Explain the educational purpose for the film's viewing and its related curriculum. Parents not wishing their children to view the film should indicate their objection on the return slip.

(Reference: Administrative Memorandum No. 48)

Granite School District   **School Closure**
School Services

Good Practice
Preparation Procedure for School Closure

1. Schools should review and revise their emergency pre-paredness manual giving special attention to:
   a. Procedures to follow in the event of a power outage.
   b. Revision of procedures for notifying parents (large numbers of working mothers).
   c. Plans when the school is open for evening activities.

2. Schools should have a battery powered radio and fresh batteries. A battery check should be part of every fire drill.

3. Elementary schools should have a liaison person assigned to go to the nearest secondary school to receive information from the bus command post, in case of a large scale communication breakdown.

4. Determine if there is justification for a decision that school cannot be maintained (reasons of safety, heating, and/or electricity, etc.).

5. The decision to close school (except in extreme emergency) can only be made by a member of the superintendency.

6. Any school closure plan should make provisions for notification of crossing guards where applicable.

7. Schools should establish a local chain of command, if principal is unavailable.

8. Once school is determined to close, media are to be contacted for public announcement by a member of the superintendency.

Granite School District   **Record Retention**
Secondary School Services

Good Practice
School Site Record Retention Schedule*

1. *Record to be Retained Permanently:*
   Attendance Records
   Audit Reports
   Deeds and Titles
   Directory of Staff
   Grant Applications
   Individual School Record of Staff Members
   Policy Records
   School Historical Records
   Serious Accidents Involving Students
   Student Transcripts

2. *Records to be Retained for Seven Years:*
   Accidents Involving Visitors
   Check Registers
   Minor Accidents Involving Students

3. *Records to be Retained for Five Years:*
   Bids and Quotes
   Confidential Reports and Records (5 years after graduation)
   District Invoices
   Purchase Orders
   Special Education Records (5 years after graduation)

4. *Records to be Retained for Four Years:*
   Bank Statements
   Canceled Checks
   Cash Receipts Registers
   Checks and Invoices
   Deposit Slips
   Fee Waiver Applications
   Leave Application Files
   Principal's Cash Reports
   P.O.'s and Receiving Reports

Receipt Books
Requisitions
Subsidiary Ledgers (4 years after being audited)
Time & Attendance Reports
Vouchers

5. *Records to be Retained for Three Years*
   Budget Reports
   Inventories
   Program Reports

6. *Records to be Retained for Two Years:*
   Building Rental Information
   Emergency Personal Leave Forms
   Equipment Maintenance Records
        (Two years after disposition of equipment)
   Letter of Recommendation

7. *Records to be Retained for one Year*
   Work Performance Evaluations (1 year after termination)

8. All nonessential records that have not specifically been covered in the sections need not be retained except for purposes of reference or exhibition.

9. The student cumulative record should be retained for three (3) years after graduation or until the student's 21st birthday, whichever comes first. The student transcript is still a permanent record.

10. All records which have exceeded the imposed retention time listed in this Good Practice may be disposed of by contacting the Director of Purchasing. He will provide service to receive the records at your school and dispose of them appropriately. This service is available in July of each year.

Please contact the Budget Office for questions about record retention.

*Permanent personnel records are maintained in the Human Resource Department at the district's central office.

Granite School District   **Student Discipline**
School Services

Good Practice
Developing an Elementary Schoolwide Discipline Plan

References: *Administrative Memoranda 6.7.17.31.61.101 Board Policy IX.D.1.2.9.15*

I. **Developing the Plan**
    A. Create a representative school Discipline Committee
        1. Teachers
        2. Parents
        3. Principal
        4. Student support services team members
        5. Students (when appropriate)
    B. Committee identifies tasks, goals, and problems to be addressed
    C. Committee develops a tentative plan
        1. Interventions
        2. Documentation
        3. Due process provisions including a review procedure
        4. Process of communication
        5. A "severe clause" that escalates intervention for severe and dangerous behaviors
    D. Plan is reviewed by Staff Team, PTA, School Services, others
    E. Revisions made as needed
    F. Plan is communicated to parents and students
    G. Plan is periodically evaluated and revisions made as needed

II. **Establishing Interventions for the Plan**
    A. Rewards/Incentives to Create a Positive School Climate (see Appendix)
    B. Systematic Instructional Programs (see Appendix)
    C. Consequences (see Appendix)
        1. Individual Counseling as each situation arises
        2. Hierarchical Systems

    D. Use of Disciplinary Suspension from School (see Administrative Memorandum #17 Pt. IV)

    E. Specific Cautions on the Use of Behavioral Interventions (see Appendix)

III. Communicating the Plan

    A. Written, Published and Distributed to Parents
1. Registration or first day packet
2. School newsletter and/or letter home
3. Back-to-School Night explanation
4. Student/Parent Handbook
5. Student or parent sign-off procedure may be helpful
6. Use of "Cottage Meetings" to explain/clarify the plan

    B. Student Instruction
1. By teachers in individual classrooms
2. In an assembly with role-playing vignettes
3. Instruction in acceptable alternative behaviors
4. Post the plan and expectations in halls, classrooms, lunchroom, etc.

IV. Other Considerations

    A. Procedures for Documentation: white slips, log books, anecdotal notes (see Memorandum #61)

    B. Procedures for Special Education Students (see Memorandum # 17)

    C. Consistency and Follow-Through are Critical

    D. Always include some provision for a degree of principal discretion for special circumstances

Granite School District   **Safe Schools**
School Services

Good Practice
Steps to Determine Need for Safe
School District Referral

References: *Administrative Memorandum 106. Board Policy Section IX-D-2*

DETERMINATION of whether violation is under Safe School Guidelines.

1. Did the incident occur on school grounds, at a school sanctioned activity, or to/from school?

2. If not, is the safety of students at school in jeopardy or the normal operations of school being disrupted?

3. If yes to one or both of the above, then consider:

   ♦ Have all primary parties been interviewed?
   ♦ Have parent conferences been held?
   ♦ Have items of evidence been confiscated or determined to exist?
   ♦ Was a law enforcement referral made?
   ♦ Have similar incidents occurred before or is student currently on a Safe Schools contract?

4. Should the incident be resolved at the school level? If the answer is no, make a district referral.

Granite School District **Student Travel**
High School Services

Good Practice
Checklist for Student Travel

1. **References:** Student Travel is addressed in the Granite School District Board of Education Policy Manual at pp. 922–924. The policy authorizes the administration to approve student travel within certain guidelines.

2. Checklist for approval of student travel requests.
   a. Is the school sponsoring, promoting, and/or collecting funds for student travel? If so, the school is responsible to cover the costs of students on fee waivers.
   b. Does the school have the financial resources to cover costs for students on fee waivers?
   c. Will fund raising activities be required? Is the fund raiser appropriate and has it received prior approval from the principal?
   d. Have issues related to school liability been examined? Have all participants submitted a written release of liability and proof of medical insurance?
   e. How many students are participating in more than one travel experience?
   f. Has the school given consideration to the objection of some parents that costs for student travel creates a financial hardship?
   g. Does the school have adequate professional leave to hire substitutes for advisors and chaperons?
   h. Does the value of the activity and its relationship to the curriculum create a compelling argument for approval?

Granite School District   **Surplus Procedures**
School Services

Good Practice
Surplus Teachers

1. Professional Agreement—Article 17
2. Time Line

Elementary Posting & Surplus Notice	Secondary Posting & Surplus Notice	Application Deadline (11 days from posting)	Hiring Deadline (Application deadline plus 10 days)	Last Elem. & Sec. Posting (Friday before June 15th)	Last day for application to Posted Vacancies	Hiring Deadline for the Last Posting	Begin Administrative Placement of Remaining Surplus
April 10	April 20	X	X + 10	June 15	June 26	July 6	July 7

3. Faculty Announcement
   a. Inform faculty that it will be necessary to surplus teachers for the next school year.
   b. Disclose known program needs and deadlines for applications.
4. Conference with Teacher(s) Who Might be Declared Surplus
   a. Review Program Needs
   b. Review Relative Qualifications
   c. Review Seniority
   d. Document Conference

5. Select the Teacher(s) You will Recommend to be Declared Surplus

6. Letter to Teacher(s) You are Recommending to be Declared Surplus
    a. State that you are recommending the teacher be declared surplus.
    b. Indicate conference date (from #3 above).
    c. Advise the teacher to apply for posted vacancies or write a letter to the Personnel Office stating placement be handled by them.
    d. Forward your recommendations by copying your School Services Administrator with this letter.

7. Administrative Placement of Surplus Teachers not Hired to Posted Vacancies by School Services and Personnel

Granite School District   **Selection Committees**
Personnel Department

Good Practice
Composition and Duties of Selection Committees
for Secretarial/classified Openings

1. "A committee of at least three persons will conduct the inter-
    view and will have an equal say as to the selected candi-
    date." *Policies, Rules and Regulations of the Board of Education,*
    p. 516.

    A. One member of the committee shall hold a position that
        is related to the position being selected.
    B. One member of the committee shall work in a depart-
        ment or school that is independent of the department or
        school where the position is being filled.

2. "A candidate's job knowledge, work performance, attitude,
    and related factors will be determined during the interview.
    The most qualified candidate will be selected. If two or more
    candidates are judged to be equally capable and qualified to
    hold the position for which they are being interviewed, de-
    partment seniority and then District seniority shall be the
    deciding factor." *Policies, Rules and Regulations of the Board of*
    Education, p. 516.

3. The selection of individuals to fill secretarial/classified po-
    sitions must be fair and aboveboard and free from "pre-
    selection." No candidate shall be promised or in any way
    given the impression that they have been selected until all
    interviews have been completed and the selected candidate
    is approved by personnel. **Evidence of "preselection" may**
    be grounds for disqualifying a particular candidate. The
    departing employee should not be involved in the interview
    process.

PRINCIPAL'S MONTHLY SCHOOL INSPECTION REPORT

The principal's monthly school inspection report is a checklist which the school principal, in company with the school custodian, uses while making a monthly walking inspection of the school plant. Specific areas of the school are visited and visually inspected. Each area is designated as

- ◆ acceptable and in good order;
- ◆ not acceptable and needing attention;
- ◆ questionable and needing specialized assistance from the district in order to determine whether the condition is acceptable or not.

If an area is designated unacceptable or questionable, the nature of the concern is noted. Work orders requesting that problem areas be fixed or looked at are completed immediately on the conclusion of the inspection tour. The date the work order is completed is entered on the inspection report form under "Action Taken/Date W.O. Submitted" and then both the inspection report and work orders are sent to the central administration.

EDUCATION LAW INTO PRACTICE

West's Education Law Reporter describes itself as "the leading school law reporting service for school boards, administrators, professors of educational law, and school attorneys." This *Reporter* contains the full text of all reported cases dealing with any aspect of education (public and private K-12 and higher education) from state appellate courts and United States District Courts. It also contains commentaries about court cases and legislation affecting education, as well as summaries or reports on empirical research related to educational law. Recently, the Reporter began printing a special section entitled *Education Law Into Practice* (ELIP), which is sponsored by the Education Law Association. The purpose of this special section, according to the *Reporter*, "is to publish short, practical pieces on topics in education law that are important to practitioners and attorneys." It is intended that "checklists, charts, sample forms, model policies, sample memoranda, sample documents, and procedural guidelines ...thoroughly supported by citations to statutes and case law" be published.

A number of very helpful and excellent pieces are being published. Most of these can be very useful to school principals and other school officials.

The range of topics treated in *Education Law Into Practice* pieces is illustrated by the following list of randomly selected authors/titles that have been published in recent issues of the Reporter.

Beckham, J. (1997). Ten judicial commandments for legally sound teacher evaluation. *West's Education Law Reporter, 119*, 331–334.

Frisby, D., and J.C. Beckham. (1998). Developing school policies on the application of reasonable force. *West's Education Law Reporter, 122*(1), 27–32.

Lynch, J.P. (1998). School districts and the Internet: Practice and model policy. *West's Education Law Reporter, 122*(1), 21–25.

Osborne, A.G. Jr. (1997). Making the manifestation determination when disciplining a special education student. *West's Education Law Reporter, 119*, 323–330.

Sorenson, G. (1997). Randi W.: When half the truth in a letter of recommendation amounts to a lie. *West's Education Law Reporter, 119*, 331–334.

Zirkel, P.A. (1998). Censoring or censuring student speech: A checklist. *West's Education Law Reporter, 121*, 477–482.

LEGAL FORM BOOKS

There are several commercial publishers that print legal form books which can be of help to school officials and lawyers working with school districts. Form books can be found in most major law libraries. One example is *American Jurisprudence Legal Forms* (2nd ed.), Vol. 16A, Chapter 229. This multivolume set of form books is published by the Lawyers Cooperative Publishing Company, Rochester, New York. Volume 16A, Chapter 229 of this set contains 450 forms pertaining to schools, school districts, administrative boards and officers, teacher and other school employees, and students. It includes model contracts, resolutions, notices, petitions, and so forth.

Legal forms extracted from form books should be scrutinized very carefully to ascertain their applicability and appropriateness for the setting and condition under consideration. School officials are encouraged to review their use with their own legal counsel. It should also be noted that a fee may be required depending on the proposed use of the form. School officials should consult the copyright page at the beginning of the form book for details or call or write the publisher.

SUGGESTED ACTIVITIES

♦ Based on your administrative experience, prepare a "good practice" policy for use by other school principals in your district.

♦ Check with your school district's insurance carrier(s) and/or state risk management office for liability prevention ideas and forms.

♦ Begin a file of *Education Into Law Practice* articles.

♦ Write one of your own *Education Into Law Practice* articles and submit it to the Education Law Association for possible publication. Manuscripts may be submitted to either of the coeditors. The coeditors at the time this book was published were:

Allan Osborne   Joseph Beckham
94 Acorn Street   Florida State University
Millis, Massachusetts 113 Stone Building
02054-1455   Tallahassee, Florida
                       32306-3021

♦ Visit a law library and review the range and types of model legal forms found in legal form books.

REFERENCES

Bounds, G.L., T.R. Trenkner, S.R. Pitcher, et al. (eds.). (1995). *American Jurisprudence legal forms* (2nd ed.). Rochester, NY: Lawyers Cooperative Publishing Company.